What *This* Katie Did

Katie Boyle

What This Katie Did

An Autobiography

Weidenfeld and Nicolson

London

The publishers are grateful for kind permission to reproduce photographs from the following sources: Keystone, 15, 25, 39; Martin Goddard, 38; Marc Henrie, 26, 29, 40; Christopher Smedley, 28; Baron, 51; Richard Dormer, 33; Richard Young, 31; *Radio Times* Picture Library, 35; Desmond O'Neill, 49; *Sun* News-papers, 52; Roderick Ebdon, 34; Paul Stokes, 37. All other photographs are from Katie Boyle's own collection. While every effort has been made to check sources, any omissions will gladly be rectified in future editions.

First published in Great Britain by
George Weidenfeld & Nicolson Ltd,
91 Clapham High Street, London sw4 7ta
1980

isbn 0 297 77814 5

Printed in Great Britain by
Butler & Tanner Ltd
Frome and London

To Margherita and Enrico
because they wanted to know
and to Peter
because I wanted him to know

Contents

List of Illustrations, ix

Strange Alliances, 1

Unconventional Schooldays, 11

A Family in Italy, 33

War and All That, 44

A Prisoner at Home, 54

Locked Away, 68

Lost and Found, 76

New Beginnings, 88

A Wife Alone, 96

Mixed Emotions, 106

Far-away Places, 114

Stars and Storms, 123

A New World, 140

Out of Step, 151

Eurovision Song Contests, 156

Anguish, 163

A Guiding Hand, 175

P.S., 188

Index, 191

Illustrations

(*between pages 22 and 23*)
My mother before her marriage
My parents' wedding
With my mother in 1927
With my nanny in Rapallo
With my father
Godmother in Rapallo
A group of my schoolfriends in England
Riding my bicycle in the grounds of Valsalice
Papa and Godmother with his prize-winning Rolls
The chapel at Valsalice where guns were hidden
Orazio Blanc, my first love
My confirmation
Grinning happily in 1938
Richard and I outside the church in 1947
My first professional modelling job
How fashions and figures change!
In the pantomime *Dick Whittington* at Windsor
Learning to sing with Bertha Nicklass Kempner

(*between pages 118 and 119*)
Greville and I on our first holiday together
Greville and I on our wedding day in 1955
A happy moment for Greville at the races
With Sugar Plum and Tai Tai
Sixteen portraits taken over the years
Three different promotional assignments
Happy times in Kenya with Greville
Greville with Girlie after his accident
Alone in a crowd, Greville and I
A late photograph of my father
Enrico, my half-brother, a few years ago
My mother and her husband, Patrick Boyle
Margherita, my half-sister, with Barouf
Sir Denis Lowson, Lord Longford and I at a party
A recent portrait by W.P. Mundy
H.M. The Queen Mother with Peter and me
Peter and I after our wedding in Lausanne

Strange
Alliances

It was September 1946. The world was a wonderful place as I bounced out of the tube at Knightsbridge. I had only been in England a month and was wearing my first grown-up hat complete with a short veil. I glanced at a young British officer striding past me and thought how smart and self-assured he looked. Suddenly he stopped, turned abruptly to face me, saluted and smiling said, 'Now I know what I have been fighting for – it was to protect pretty girls like you.' With that he turned on his heel and was gone as quickly as he had appeared. When I reached the Basil Street Hotel, I rushed to tell Mama. She had a marvellous sense of the ridiculous and put up her hands in mock horror: 'Oh! whatever would he have said if he had known your background.' My 'protector' might not have flattered me so much had he realized that while he was fighting I was at school in Italy, proudly wearing my Piccola Italiana uniform. With its black skirt, white shirt and black tie, it was the young girls' equivalent to the uniform of the Fascist Youth movement, and I had marched with zeal to Fascist songs. If he had known that my mother, accompanied by a Roman lawyer and two psychiatrists, had only recently extricated me from imprisonment in a mental home in Italy he most certainly would have reserved his touching tribute for a more suitable maiden.

But I'm getting ahead of myself; perhaps I should go back a few years, back to Italy where I was born among those lovely Tuscan hills surrounding Florence. I started life as Caterina Irene Elena Maria

I

Imperiali di Francavilla; my father was half-Neapolitan and half-Russian, and my mother half-English and half-Australian. As the product of that alliance you can understand why I can laugh, cry, swear and blush simultaneously in three languages.

My father was the Marchese Demetrio Imperiali dei Principi di Francavilla, and two full-size tombstones do his name justice in the cemetery De Pully outside Lausanne in Switzerland, where he was buried in 1962. His father was the Marchese Enrico Imperiali who, on a trip to Russia, fell in love with Katia Hvoshinsky, a daughter of Prince and Princess Hvoshinsky-Gortchakov; but family rumour has it that he intimidated her into marriage only after he had threatened to burn down her family home if she refused. The Imperialis settled in Naples and in due course produced two sons, Sacha and Valodia, and one daughter, Maroussia; then fifteen years later, as an afterthought, another son – my father – who, thanks to his mother, was soon called Mitia, the diminutive of the Russian version of his name. He grew up to be tall and fair with an over abundance of Latin exuberance and Slav charm.

Mama started life as plain Dorothy Kate Ramsden. Her father, Robert Ramsden, was a solicitor in Huddersfield who fell in love with Kate Holland, a visiting Australian beauty, and somehow she never got back to Adelaide. Unfortunately Grandfather Ramsden died suddenly of a heart attack at an early age, leaving a broken-hearted widow, and two children, my mother and her brother Jim, who was ten years older. Grandmother Ramsden had never really taken to life in a small Yorkshire town and had always wanted to travel, so when my mother was just seventeen they left Huddersfield for good and set off for her first love – Italy – leaving Jim behind.

Florence at that time, in the early twenties, was an acknowledged centre of international society. There was an invasion of American and English families with attractive daughters and preying mothers, who had their eyes set firmly on Italy's Golden Youth, especially the ones with titles. These young men often proved an expensive investment – a well-known Italian expression described them as *Miseria e Nobilta* (Impoverished Nobility). Mama, pretty as a picture, infiltrated this English/American/Italian scene with no difficulty whatsoever. With dark auburn hair, black-fringed green eyes, fair skin

and a lovely figure she was a copybook Pocket Venus, and a pleasantly padded bank balance enhanced her appeal.

When Demetrio met Dorothy it was 'love at first sight'. Nobody
was surprised by this, and apart from the gnashing of teeth of some
of Papa's ex-girlfriends, everyone smiled on their engagement.
Along with her charm and beauty she brought a nice little dowry,
whilst he contributed an attractive name complete with a coronet.
They made a very handsome couple. I would have loved to have
been at the wedding. An incongruous hotch-potch of people were
there: Uncle Arthur Ramsden, determined not to be overawed, duly
arrived from Yorkshire to give his niece away; the Russian and
Australian mothers (both Catherines) no doubt shed a sentimental
tear together and all sorts of Latins ensured it was a lively occasion.
After the honeymoon they settled down in Villa Fiorita near Fiesole
to start their married life.

I am sure they were genuinely in love, but if you think oil and
water don't mix, believe me they blend happily compared to these
two. Language differences did not help matters either. Although my
father already spoke five languages fluently, his English in those days
wasn't so hot and this caused an explosion during the only trip they
made to Yorkshire together. Over, of all things . . . table mats. Unfortunately in Italian the word 'matto' means mad, and my father,
getting hold of the wrong end of the stick, thought they were dubbing him as nutty as a fruit cake. With a roar of rage he tipped up
the heavily-laden table, and if the thought had never crossed their
minds that he might be mad, they must have begun to wonder.

My parents did, however, have some happy times together.
Although shy and undoubtedly conventional, Mama was lively
and intelligent. She became very popular in Florence, made a
number of life-long friends and enjoyed her nickname of 'the little
Marchesa'. Papa was a flamboyant, larger-than-life character who,
although oblivious to most normal social conventions, played host
with great panache and charm.

After a couple of miscarriages, Mama took to her *chaise longue*,
when she knew I was on the way, with a seraphic smile and a mountain of books. Extremely well-read, she had a passion for history, and
she stayed with her books until I was ready to be born. My goodness,

3

how modern doctors would quite rightly frown upon such a passive pregnancy.

I was born at the Villa Fiorita in the Tuscany hills and a few weeks later was baptized in Giotto's famous baptistry in Florence. Dante was baptized there and I'm sure Mama said a prayer that there might be a gift left behind for me. My godparents were all eminently suitable: amongst them was H.R.H. Princess Irene of Greece, sister of King Paul and aunt of the present King Constantine. She was a most conscientious godmother, writing encouraging letters throughout my schooldays and always remaining a very real friend to my mother. Other members of the Greek Royal Family were also close friends and often shared in the hazardous family rows that became part of our daily life. Both my mother and father had very strong characters and the incompatibility between them was bound to breed trouble. Clashes came loud and strong quite early in the marriage. I can't have been more than four when, entranced, I watched Queen Sophie act as a buffer to an enormous cushion which came flying through a door, accompanied by the usual bilingual screams and shouts from my parents. On this, as on similar occasions, I was scooped up by a passing nanny and deposited well beyond the line of fire. I often missed the fun. I'd have loved to have seen Her Majesty, Princess Irene and Mama emerge from a broom cupboard where, scared stiff, all three of them had taken refuge during a ferocious thunderstorm.

My Italian volatility and Russian romanticism have both proved useful, but I'm quite sure I would never have bounced back against the blows that life has dealt me if it had not been for my strong streak of Yorkshire stock.

The more personal but spectacular storms, rows and raised voices never scared me at all – I was fascinated. But I do have more peaceful memories of a green-shuttered white villa with rust-coloured striped awnings that were let down on hot summer days and kept the large rooms shaded and deliciously cool. There was the scent of honeysuckle everywhere.

Smells have always played an important part in my life. I loved hugging my father because he always smelt so nice. He'd clasp me in a bear-hug and I'd nuzzle into his neck and breathe in deeply. As a treat he used to take the stoppers out of his multi-coloured bottles in the bathroom, but it wasn't until years later that I noticed that there were large bottles of Arpège – the scent as well as the *eau de toilette* – yet nobody could have been more masculine than he was. After all these years Arpège is still my favourite scent.

Early memories of my mother are bound up with Molyneux Cinq and of her wafting in to kiss me goodnight in a cloud of pale green chiffon. I wasn't allowed to hug her too enthusiastically – she always put her hand up to her hair to protect it – but she smelt so good too.

Then there were happy holidays when I was very young. These were spent by the sea. Princesses, duchesses, marchesas and the rest would gather up their broods and set off, complete with nannies and lady's maids, to Viareggio, Forte dei Marmi or some similar resort. And there, in embryonic form, members of today's jet set and pillars of the establishment from all over the world would play, paddle and squabble over spades and sandcastles. A smarting memory of that time is of one small boy, now an ambassador, leaning over the tea-table and saying 'What a long neck you have, Caterinella' – this could have prompted my love of polo-neck sweaters and cover-up neck-laces. Another vivid memory is of the children's birthday party when an alcoholic or insensitive chef had soaked the cake in Kirsch – maybe it was this that put me off alcohol for life.

It's odd how erratically memory buds explode. I recall certain inci-dents with staggering clarity, whilst others that people try and remind me of mean absolutely nothing. For example, I was about five years old when my parents separated and I can't remember much about that, but some very fast car rides stick vividly in my mind. Apparently Mama and Papa took it in turns to kidnap me and I was always bundled into the back of a car, told to lie down and a dark rug was draped over me. This rug was the only thing I objected to because I wanted to see what was going on. I thoroughly enjoyed all the excitement.

Children are supposed to be emotionally battered and bruised when their parents divorce. I must have been either a very balanced and adaptable child or an extremely callous one; perhaps because I was born under the twin sign of Gemini, I like to think it was the former. Anyway it wasn't long before I realized that, although I genuinely adored both my parents, I could play one off against the other and get the best from each of them. The only time, in fact, that my mother ever lost her temper with me was when I must have pushed this tactic a bit too far. In quick succession she threw a telephone, a hairbrush and a vase at me. I deserved to be hit by each of them – and I was.

I cannot believe that it was in the hope of making me a better girl, but about this time I was taken for an audience with the Pope. At that tender age the Vatican made little impression on me, but the Pope's ring, and the smell of incense and garlic, are details I have not forgotten. A very short while after this visit, I went down with scarlet fever. Whether this was due to a Vatican germ or not, it was a bad attack and when I came out of the Anglo-American Hospital in Rome I could hardly use my left leg. Nanny took me to Sorrento to convalesce and I was made to ride a tricycle every day. Oh! how I cried with frustration; because of that weak leg, all I could do was to go round and round in circles.

It wouldn't be fair to write another word without pointing out that my father was a Fascist. To him Fascism spelt patriotism and he loved his country intensely. Papa associated himself with Mussolini because he genuinely believed that only through him would Italy be able to solve her problems – and for a number of years this undoubtedly proved to be the case. In his lapel my father always wore the small 1922 badge which commemorated his part in the Fascist march on Rome. It was still there when he was amongst those who greeted General Alexander in Turin after the war, and I am proud to say that he was one of the few Italians who never denied that he had been a Fascist in the original and best sense of the word.

It was in his capacity of Vice Federale of Florence that Papa represented the Duce at Sir Walter Becker's funeral in the English cemetery just outside Florence. Nobody could have guessed at the time that Lady Becker was soon to become my first stepmother. Sir Walter Becker, a British shipping tycoon, had built his fortune in Italy over the eighty or so years of his life. He idolized his wife Delphine, who was twenty-five years younger than he, and they were very happy but, despite many miscarriages, they never had the children they longed for. Sir Walter was greatly respected in Turin, but regarded as an eccentric. He was a familiar figure, elegant, with a white beard and a rose in his button-hole, walking daily to his office, followed a few feet behind by his chauffeur-driven car. When he died, his widow was left a very rich woman indeed.

Not long after the funeral an attachment began to form between my father and Lady Becker. He was only thirty and she very nearly sixty, but I don't like to think it was only the glint of gold that appealed to him: she was still a very attractive woman, chic, with soft grey hair, a sweet smile and great presence. On the other hand, I do know that he waited to make his proposal until he had discovered who held the purse-strings – Delphine or her pretty young niece Mireille. There were many rumours flying around at the time, but with my young eyes I saw a lot of love between this unlikely couple.

It was because Papa and Lady Becker got married that I became Hungarian. As they made their plans, the important detail of his divorce from my mother had to be settled; there being no such thing as divorce in Italy, the only way round this problem was for him to take a different nationality. Hungary appeared to be a hospitable and uncritical country, so it was the one he chose, and when he became Hungarian he made a point of having my name added to his passport. This no doubt was done to infuriate my mother, who he knew was very anxious to have me become a naturalized British citizen. As soon as he could he had my Hungarian nationality confirmed, so I was issued with my own smart green and gold Magyar passport on which I travelled until I was married.

It is still a moot point as to whether Mama and Papa were completely divorced when he and Delphine Becker set off for Budapest – but that was a minor problem. By coincidence, my father had adopted the Hungarian name of a man wanted by the police for a serious crime. Their boarding of the wagon-lit, preceded by Delphine's personal maid bearing pink satin sheets for their bunks and brand-new matching luggage, could hardly have passed unnoticed, so it was not surprising that half-way through the night there was a loud knocking on the door. Papa's 'Come in' revealed four formidable policemen who demanded to see his passport. With no trace

7

of guilt he showed it to them – only to find himself grasped by the shoulders, escorted down the corridor still in his pyjamas and dressing-gown, pushed into a police car and taken off to a cell in a Hungarian jail. The romantic journey took an unpleasant turn, particularly as Papa had no documents, other than his new passport with the adopted name, to prove his identity. The situation was smoothed out the next day, but those first few hours had given the love-birds a nasty shock. Their quiet wedding took place as soon as possible in Budapest, and they made their way back to Italy.

As wedding-presents, Delphine gave my father not only a Rolls Royce, but also a convertible Lancia Dilambda. These two cars had to be very special ones, of course, so Papa set off in search of an equally special car designer. A young man called Pinin Farina impressed him greatly, and to the then unknown youngster he gave the double commission. Mr Farina, who was to become *the* name in car design, did him proud – he produced two beautiful cars. The Rolls won the Grand Prix d'Honneur at the 1936 Monte Carlo Grand Prix and the Dilambda carried off the first prize in the same year.

I now had my first stepmother, who provided both my father and myself with two beautiful new homes, Valsalice (Willow Valley) near Turin and a villa near Rapallo on the Ligurian Riviera. There is no doubt that Delphine de Martelly Becker (she was half-French and half-English) influenced my young life and the formation of my ideas and principles more than anyone else. The enormous difference in our ages didn't seem to matter at all to either of us; she established immediate contact with me and I warmed to her at once. First of all we had to decide what I would call her. We agreed we disliked the 'Aunt' label with which even strangers were often tagged. Then, possibly thinking of the two new homes, I piped up, 'Will you be giving me things?'

'Yes,' she replied cautiously – perhaps I had touched on a delicate point for any rich woman – 'I suppose I shall give you a present for your birthday and at Christmas.'

'Then I could call you my Fairy Godmother.'

'But won't that be an awful mouthful for you to say every time we talk? How about just "Godmother"?' So Godmother she became. I loved her dearly, admired her tremendously, and through all the difficult times we encountered together she earned my undying devotion.

My father was always begging me to be gentle with her because, rather like an exuberant puppy, I flung myself into her arms whenever I saw her. But, as I got older and grew taller than she, I became more gentle and protective. Godmother always had time for me. In the school holidays, as a special treat, we would set off to what we called the 'spoil the appetite' shops: little restaurants in Piazza San Carlo where we would have an innocent aperitif and she would allow me to nibble sweet and savoury canapés. These did nothing to dull my healthy greed at meal-times, but the trips made me feel so grown-up and created an even greater bond between us. Then there were our 'talk-abouts'. When at Rapallo, we would stroll up and down the terrace of Villa Delmitia (a blending of both their names), which overlooked the Mediterranean not far below. We talked about everything, sometimes until way past dusk when the moon would start to rise over the sea and bats skimmed over our heads in the twilight. I could always tell Godmother anything; she shared my hopes, my joys and my fears, and I would listen absorbed as she told me about her early life; of when she was a lonely young schoolteacher at Rolle in Switzerland; of how she had found three roses of encouragement by her bed one evening, put there by the headmistress; and of how she met and married Walter Becker. We came to know each other so very well.

This close relationship of ours didn't mean, however, that Godmother wasn't strict with me. Although always fair, she was a great believer in discipline. One thing she insisted on was that I should learn how to make my own bed (with hospital-style corners) as well as clean my room and my bath. Despite the considerable number of servants in the house I was never expected to ring a bell for one myself. Godmother's sensible motto was: 'You must not give an order unless you know how to do the task as well, or better, yourself.' For this attitude, too, I shall always be grateful to this remarkable woman – at least I know I shall always be able to earn my living as a housekeeper.

Unconventional Schooldays

My schooldays were not entirely happy but they were eventful. Of the six schools I was sent to, I was expelled from four – hardly a virtuous record. It's not that I was an out-and-out rebel but I was very lively and had an individual approach to discipline. I never could see why rules couldn't be slightly bent. In a way I thought they were there to test our skill in breaking them. Adaptable from birth, I didn't really mind where I was sent and I was always prepared to settle down quite happily. The basic trouble was probably that, from an early age, I always wanted something 'to be going on' and when nothing was, I had to make it happen.

My education was set against the backcloth of bitter squabbles between my parents. Each wanted me to stay in their own country so, as a compromise and to avoid bloodshed, I was sent in turn to schools in England and Italy, with Switzerland thrown in as neutral ground. Reluctantly, my father gave my mother first choice. At the time, she was living in the South of France for six months of the year in order to make the most of what my father had left her of her income. She wanted me to go to England, so it was my Australian grandmother, Gaggie, who was left as it were 'holding the baby'.

Gaggie had eventually returned to England and had bought a small cottage on the Aldwick Bay Estate near Bognor Regis. Gaggie herself was a small tubby woman with a predilection for white satin blouses which I always slid off when I hugged her. Then there was

Gaggie's wonderful Yorkshire terrier, Joey, and together we played and paddled in a very cold sea. I had never lived in a cottage before and it felt very small after all the space I had been used to.

I was enrolled at the Apsley House School for Girls. I had never been to school before but I liked it immediately. I shall never forget the two sisters who ran the school, but only have blurred memories of lacrosse and the disappointment of not being allowed to be in the end-of-term play. I did not have time to settle down though, because suddenly a feud flared up between my parents, and it was goodbye Bognor and hello Broadstairs.

North Foreland Lodge was considered to be the *crème de la crème*, as Miss Brodie would say, both socially and scholastically. Miss Fennella Gammell, the headmistress, was certainly in a class of her own. She was a tall, dark, strikingly-handsome woman with hair swept back into a bun at the nape of her neck; her voice was soft and she commanded respect on sight. Papa, with his well-trained eye for a pretty woman, took a great shine to her. He even stopped ranting and raving about 'my Italian daughter being sent to another blasted English school'.

I really could not be blamed for the first incident at North Foreland. It would never have taken place if my Father had not insisted that I should have a bedroom to myself. He always seemed to want me to feel that I was a person apart. Anyway, one evening, just as I was dropping off to sleep, my door handle slowly began to turn. Then, by degrees, the door was pushed open. One of the 'big' girls shut the door silently behind her and, smiling, walked towards my bed.

Stockily-built, with broad shoulders and arms too long for her body, she had straight, chin-length hair and I noticed her regular, very white teeth as she smiled. Her eyes held mine as she came closer. I pulled up the sheet to my chin, but she took no notice and sat down very close to me. She said nothing – neither did I. Then gently and very slowly she leant over and pressed her lips on mine. It was so unexpected that I started to scream but her hand clamped firmly across my mouth to muffle any sound. 'You little idiot,' she hissed, 'it would have been such fun.' And with that she was gone. I was bewildered – I was barely ten years old and the sensual side of life

12

was still a closed book. Puberty is such a sensitive, vulnerable stage of one's life, but at that moment and in retrospect, my reactions were instinctively heterosexual.

The second incident at the school was, however, entirely caused by me. Being an avid film fan, I used to smuggle in every movie magazine I could lay my hands on. I identified in turn with Joan Crawford, Katherine Hepburn, Ava Gardner etc., always those women with high cheek bones and slender faces, never a smiling, chubby-faced blonde. I'd spend hours in front of a looking-glass, drawing in my cheeks and admiring the hollowed effect. My plan, when I grew up, was to go to Hollywood and have all my back teeth pulled out – I'd read somewhere that that was what Joan Crawford had done to achieve those lovely facial lights and shades. And so I went on dreaming; indeed, so much so that I told my young classmates the most ludicrous story: I was none other than Annabella, wife of film-star Tyrone Power (he was the rage at that time starring as Ferdinand de Lesseps in the film *Suez* and Annabella was playing opposite him). How anyone could have been taken in by my fiction for even one minute amazes me and I do not really think it was that which caused all the trouble – I had to go one step further and threaten to slit the wrist or throat of any girl who dared to go and 'tell on me' to Miss Gammell. I even brought out a pocket-knife to show that I meant business. Of course, one brave young thing went straight to Miss Gammell and told her.

All hell was let loose: first I was called to the headmistress's study, then I was 'sent to Coventry'. My bedroom door was locked at night and it was not long before my mother and father appeared – for once together. There were no smiles, no endearments and I left North Foreland Lodge in the back seat of a large car sandwiched between Papa and Mama, who sat in silence all the way back to London.

My whole world seemed terribly muddled. The next thing I remember was the gloomy grandeur of a large room and an impressive gentleman who spoke with a guttural accent; he turned out to be a Harley Street psychiatrist. He sat me in a leather chair which was slippery and the touch of it set my teeth on edge – I have been unable to sit comfortably on leather furniture ever since. He sat behind a massive desk, planted his elbows, fingertips touching, and leant forward. His beady eyes bored into me from behind his horn-rimmed glasses. The silence unnerved me. Then he asked, 'Do you love your mother and father?'

'Of course,' I whispered, 'what a silly question.'

'Do you enjoy sausages?'

'Yes, quite.'

'And bananas.'

I saw no connection. 'Yes,' I said again.

Could there really have been phallic undertones? Of course, I didn't understand, but I do know that when I repeated these questions to Papa, he raced back to Harley Street and threatened violence. What actually happened I never did find out, but the final cryptic word came from the psychiatrist: 'Having got to know the father, I have nothing but understanding for the daughter.' For once in our lives there was a strong solidarity between my father and myself – but this incident ended my short sojourn at North Foreland Lodge.

Next came Brillantmont, set high above Lausanne on Switzerland's Lake Leman and divided into Château and Villa. Brillantmont was run by two sisters, Madame Huguenin and Mademoiselle Heubi, helped by Monsieur Huguenin. The Villa specialized in Domestic Sciences and was, strictly speaking, a finishing school; the Château took in younger children and, as I was going on eleven, I was amongst '*les petites*' – the little ones.

Parents sent their children to Brillantmont from all parts of the world. There was always a generous sprinkling of Americans, British and Europeans galore. It was, in fact, a glorious cosmopolitan blend, and the whole place had a lilt of luxury about it. During my spell there, minor royalty was represented by Princess Olga de Hesse, and the British Ambassador Winant's three attractive daughters were amongst the many offspring of the diplomatic service. World-famous Bach pianist Borovski's daughter Natasha became a close friend of mine, and Gertrude Lawrence and Marlene Dietrich had entrusted their daughters Pamela and Maria to the establishment. There was always great excitement when famous relatives came to call and my whole stay was highlighted on the day Miss Dietrich stepped out of her chauffeur-driven Rolls dressed in the palest grey

– I swore I would never wear any other colour – and leant on the mudguard of her car signing autographs. As she left, her fox stole brushed against me. Memories are made of this for a screen-struck youngster.

I loved being at Brillantmont and enthusiastically threw myself into everything that was happening. During the Spring and Summer terms we played tennis, swam and rode horses through the woods. It was during one of these rides on a magnificent white horse that a roving amateur photographer took a picture of me to enter for a competition. It must have won because, to my father's horror, he picked up a Swiss magazine in Italy and saw me beaming out at him over the caption, 'Beauty and the Beast'. There was much rumbling from him about slack discipline, but I was delighted with my first cover shot.

At Brillantmont I did at least learn French. I'd learnt some at home from Nonna (my French-speaking Russian grandmother) but I fear I acquired a Russian 'R' from her which I have never been able to lose. However, it was at Brillantmont that I developed a convenient crush on our good-looking French master. Monsieur Fremont made me determined to speak the language so I clung to every word of his French lesson and luckily a good deal of it clung to me. By the time I got home after the first term I was able to chatter away in French, much to the surprise and delight of everyone.

As a bonus for having learnt French, Papa decided to take me back to Brillantmont via Paris, even though this was a long detour. When we walked into the George v Hotel, a tall, willowy blonde glided towards us.

'Mitia darlink, I thought you would never get here!'

I gawped as she pressed her lips to Papa's. Her voice was low, she sounded Scandinavian and she obviously expected us.

'This is Steena, Caterinella, and I want you both to be friends,' said my father.

My heart sank. I'd been longing for this trip to Paris alone with Papa – I always loved the way all doors opened to him, the fuss everyone made of him – and the thought of being able to bask in his reflected glamour and have him all to myself, was something I'd been building up in my mind for weeks. Now this had to happen. Well, at least she was very pretty and I wasn't really going to let anything dampen my enthusiasm.

Although I was only eleven, I felt so grown-up as we were escorted to our suite. Two bedrooms with huge beds and a sitting-room in the middle overlooked the tree-lined Avenue George v. For our first lunch we had caviare (I loved it), champagne (I didn't), and crêpes Suzettes still brilliantly aflame as they touched my plate. Papa reached for Steena's hand – she drew it away and smoothed my cheek with it instead.

The Eiffel Tower, the Sacré Coeur and later a visit to the Louvre. I was still agog with energy – Steena and Papa a little less so.

'What about a little rest?' they suggested.

'Oh, yes,' I said. 'Let's go to a cinema!'

They looked at each other and we set off to see *Snow White and the Seven Dwarfs*. I thought I saw Papa and Steena holding hands, but was far too engrossed in the screen to worry about it. After the movie we sat in a café on the Champs-Élysées and had some more delicious things to eat and drink. I knew Papa's leg was pressed hard against Steena's.

'Aren't you even a little bit tired?' asked my father hopefully.

'Not at all, Papa. What are we going to do now?' I was equally hopeful. 'Another cinema?'

Watches were consulted and the idea of giving me an early dinner, then leaving me at the hotel, was quickly set aside, 'Because, Papa, you promised I could stay up really late, and it is my one and only night in Paris, probably till I am very old.'

As we went in to see Clark Gable and Claudette Colbert in *It Happened One Night*, I tucked my arm under my father's, 'You see, Papa, I am also learning a lot more French by going to the cinema,' I whispered.

With hindsight, it must have been hell for my poor father: a dreadful conflict between lust and duty. He was obviously dying to get this gorgeous girl between the sheets, and by now it was beginning to show. If the movie was great, the entertainment next to me was even greater. Their hands seemed to be all over each other, and if the sound-track was loud, their breathing was even louder. This was great stuff. I never imagined Paris would be like this. Suddenly I thought of Godmother. I had eavesdropped once, and overheard her say, 'Mitia darling, I do know how much older I am than you, so I will understand if you stray once in a while.' This, I thought, must have been what she meant by straying.

It was late enough for anyone to dine by the time we got out from this second movie, and again my appetite did credit to the huge meal. This time it included duck at the Tour d'Argent. It was so delicious that, for a few minutes, it even dulled my interest in what Steena and Papa were going to do next.

At last, by the time the taxi dropped us back at the hotel, I was wilting. But when I was all tucked up and kissed goodnight, my curiosity got the better of me. I just had to have a look and see what those two were going to get up to now that they had finally got rid of me. I crept out of bed, and very quietly opened the door to Papa's bedroom. The lights were low – I could see my father standing there without a stitch of clothing – but what on earth was that sticking out in front of him? Then, outlined by the light from the bathroom, came the slim, long-legged and bare figure of Steena. She went towards him, and together they slowly sank back onto the bed. I wanted so badly to keep watching, but my eyelids were very heavy and some instinct told me that this was the time to close the door and go back to bed. My last thought that night was, if Godmother did not mind, why should I?

Just as my mind took willingly to French, it stalled over German. No amount of private lessons or hearing it spoken at home got me far beyond the basics. On another occasion, therefore, my father took me back to Brillantmont via Berlin, and from the moment we left Valsalice he spoke only German to me.

My general impression of Berlin was that it was full of formidably fat women and bustling jovial men. I had never seen so many cake-shops, and even now every time I go back, I make for those delicious mid-morning fumes of foaming hot chocolate.

After a busy 'educative' day, we were sitting in the hotel lounge, and I remember thinking what a totally different feel it had from its Parisian counterpart, when my eyes came to a halt on a group of striking women: two blondes and a brunette, all three outstandingly chic, having a drink with a young man. My father had seen them too, and he asked the hotel manager, who was passing the time of day with us, who they were.

'Nobody in particular,' he replied.

'I would very much like to meet them,' said Papa, and I felt that my German was about to progress.

'No, I do not think that would be a good idea.' The manager was adamant; my father taken aback.

'I still feel it would be kind of you to arrange an introduction,' insisted Papa.

'They are not for you, Sir, but as you wish, of course.' You could have cracked the ice between them by now.

The whole atmosphere of this trip was completely different from our Paris outing, and after an early dinner Papa put me to bed and said goodnight. I don't know how long I had been asleep, but I woke with a start to hear the sitting-room door open. He was back and he was not alone. Wide awake by now, I heard the champagne cork pop and curiosity forced me out of bed to see who was there. It was Papa with the two blondes. This time they looked even more stunning in full evening dress, draped in jewels and furs.

My curiosity satisfied, I went back to bed. I had had enough German for the day. But in a matter of minutes, roars of rage echoed through the rooms, followed by squawks and screams. Suddenly my door crashed open and a bald man, clutching a long blonde wig and the remains of his glamour clothes, hurtled past my bed, skidded and crashed to the floor. The second blonde raced through after him, followed by my father, who seemed to pick up one in each hand, and hurl them into the corridor, bellowing after them in German.

He turned, slammed the door, then realized I was there.

'Don't you ever mention this to anyone,' he growled. 'Go to sleep and I will see you in the morning.'

I never did tell on him, but years later I heard him tell the story against himself, in more vivid detail, helpless with laughter.

After I was expelled from Brillantmont – for what I considered to be a most unfair verdict over my participation in a midnight feast – Mama and Papa began to wonder what to do with their daughter. Things got so bad that my mother even came and spent the night at Valsalice under the same roof as Papa and Godmother.

We all got on quite happily between those long sessions when my parents went into a huddle behind closed doors to discuss my future education. We all – Godmother, Mama and Papa – played with the dogs on the lawn. Then there was lunch when sparks nearly flew between my parents and Godmother brought them quietly to order with 'Now children, you two must behave!' At last my parents were in full agreement that after the somewhat sophisticated atmosphere of Brillantmont, I need a more restrained environment. My father won hands down in his argument against English schools and Swiss compromises so they agreed that I should stay in Italy.

While a final decision was being made, Godmother and Papa, who were both determined that I should appreciate 'good music', took me to the Maggio Fiorentino for a week. They had already added to the groundwork of their musical evenings at Valsalice by taking me to the open-air opera house in Turin's Valentino Gardens where I enjoyed Verdi, Mozart, Smetana and many others (I dropped off during Wagner); and of course, the ever-active radiogram in our ball-room poured out Dvořák dances, Russian choruses, Bach and Beethoven. A catholic hotchpotch if ever there was one, to which I added, to my father's horror, a definite liking for Vera Lynn, Anne Shelton and Bing Crosby. In an attempt to prevent a serious deterioration in my taste we attended the musical gathering in Florence which attracted music-lovers from all over the world. Artists, famous and aspiring, flocked there to perform. This particular Maggio Fiorentino was the last before the war forced the event out of existence.

We stayed at the Excelsior Hotel; so did a lot of the stars. Beniamino Gigli, rotund and dapper, wearing a black homburg hat, white gloves and carrying a black cane, reached Reception as we did. His entourage included his daughter, and there seemed to be some mix-up over their booking. Our suite, apparently, was sandwiched between their two. My Father offered to switch so they would be in adjoining rooms and ruffled feathers were smoothed; what was more, to my delight, we had achieved an immediate introduction. Our relationship was put under a certain strain, though, because every time Miss Gigli soared the scales in the room next door to ours, Godmother's two pekes joined in with loud, determined harmonizing. I think the honours were even and no feelings hurt because when my father offered apologies, the Great Gigli asked us if we would like to go to a rehearsal of *La Bohème* – he was singing Rodolfo, of course.

For me this was, without a doubt, the highlight of the Maggio Fiorentino. They could keep their lavish 'end products' of *Il Ballo in Maschera* and *Traviata*, even *La Bohème* meant less to me when the curtain rose before an elegantly-dressed audience. That empty theatre with the house lights on, the curtain open on a half-lit stage, the hollow sound of footsteps on the bare boards, the interruptions in the middle of arias, the singers rehearsing in everyday clothes – all this to me was Magic. I think it was at that moment that I slotted deep into my mind the determination, and not merely the dream, that one day, somehow, somewhere, I would have something to do with this dusty but devastatingly attractive world of Show Business. It mattered not one iota that I'd shown no talent whatsoever for singing, dancing or acting, and that my background was ludicrously far removed from such a world. I just knew I would find a way.

At that time, though, all I had was a flamboyant father, and even on this occasion he didn't take a back seat. When Gigli stopped singing, Papa's voice could still be heard continuing the aria from the stalls.

'Marchese,' called out the tenor. 'You have a good voice. Come up on the stage and we will sing together.'

The duet between Marcello and Rodolfo, '*O Mimi Tu Piu Non Torni*', has never sounded quite the same to me since, and probably to nobody else who was there either.

With no difficulty at all, I can transport myself back into that theatre. I can smell it, hear the voices and unashamedly wallow in the tunefulness of Puccini.

Back to reality. On our return home I was told that my new school had been chosen and I was delivered to the Collegio Cabrini. The convent, built high on the hills above Genoa, had a magnificent view of the port. Perhaps the family chose this school on purpose because Nonna, my Russian grandmother who lived nearby at Via Antonio Crocco, with her efficient little pouter-pigeon-shaped housekeeper, Adelina, had a full view of the school playing-fields from her drawing-room window.

Cabrini was certainly a great contrast to Brillantmont. Discipline was rigid. We moved about the school in silent crocodiles, accompanied everywhere by at least one nun. The nuns glided rather than walked, and I learnt that it was wiser to take heed of what they said. A raised eyebrow or a glance immediately restored order if we transgressed.

It was at Cabrini that I was first introduced to an excellent breakfast: the yolk of an egg in a mug, covered with sugar and stirred to a smooth cream. This was topped up with weak piping hot *café au lait*, frothing it up deliciously.

I took my first Communion at the Cabrini – very late for a Catholic as I was twelve. There were six of us sharing this important day, and we approached it with genuine reverence and excitement. However, it was ruined for me by the fact that, in comparison with the flat virginal fronts of the other girls, I was already remarkably well-developed. However hard I tried to camouflage the two big bulges which showed through the simple straight white communion dress I failed miserably. So I walked down the aisle, head lowered, hands devoutly clasped and shoulders hunched forward as far as possible to try and disguise my embarrassing bosom.

I think I behaved reasonably well at this school, and even got good marks for my schoolwork. My troubles, never far away, returned when I got a letter to tell me that Godmother and Papa were off to America, so I wouldn't be going home for the summer holidays. Instead, I was to go with a group of nuns, and other girls who for some reason were not going home either, to an annexe of Cabrini, a villa by the sea at Bellaria on the Adriatic coast.

That holiday was a great change for me because for once I had children of my own age to play with. For the first time too I fell under the spell of a handsome young beachcomber. A fleeting romance flared as we exchanged glances on the beach under the hot sun, and he sang love songs to me to the accompaniment of his guitar under my window at night. It was my first experience of love under a summer moon and I romantically enjoyed it to the full.

The nuns, though, were not slow to tell my father of this incident and once again I was under a cloud. It is incredible to think that this innocent episode made the school feel that I might be maturing too fast for them to cope. But there it is – I never did go back that autumn for the new scholastic year. Of course I had written to Mama and told her of my troubles so she arranged for me to go and spend a fortnight with her in London before deciding on a new school. We were now in late August 1939; I was just at an age to remember riding in Rotten Row, feeding the ducks on the Serpentine, going to the Zoo, and the pleasant flat in Dorchester Court, just in the middle of Sloane Street. I enjoyed every minute of life in London. Then suddenly everything changed. The telephone rang non-stop at all times of the day and night. My mother seemed to be locked in endless earnest conversations with visitors I'd never seen before. Doors were shut if ever I was within earshot; the word 'war' cropped up all the time, and then my father arrived unexpectedly looking fierce and forceful.

'Mitia, promise you won't leave me without any news. You do realize that I am only letting her go because I feel you and Delphine are in a better position to look after her, don't you?' These *cris de coeur* I shall never forget. My mother's voice rose higher and higher, her eyes were always red and she cried a lot. As she packed my suitcase she often clasped me to her so tightly that I felt I would suffocate. 'You won't forget me, will you, my darling? I love you so much.' My feelings mangled, I knew something dreadful was happening but I could not quite gather what. Then one morning my father came to collect me and the suitcases were loaded into a taxi. All three of us got in. 'Victoria Station, please.' We arrived and I clung to my mother's hand. We hugged yet again. 'Dorothy, please stop crying, you're making it far worse for the child.' He led me firmly up the platform to the Golden Arrow. Travelling in this train had always been the most tremendous treat for me, but today was very different. As the train drew out of the station I could see nothing through my tears except the blurred small figure of my mother with a crumpled hankie pressed to her face.

Poggio Imperiale in Florence is an impressive-looking school. Built originally by one of the Dukes of Lorraine for his mistress in the seventeenth century it stands at the top of the hill leading from the Porta Romana. With the Viale dei Colli and Piazzale Michelangelo

ABOVE My mother before her marriage
ABOVE RIGHT My parents' wedding

BELOW With my mother in 1927
BELOW RIGHT Me with my nanny in Rapallo

ABOVE LEFT With my father
ABOVE RIGHT Godmother in Rapallo

At school in England; I am, of course, the one holding the dog

In the grounds of Valsalice

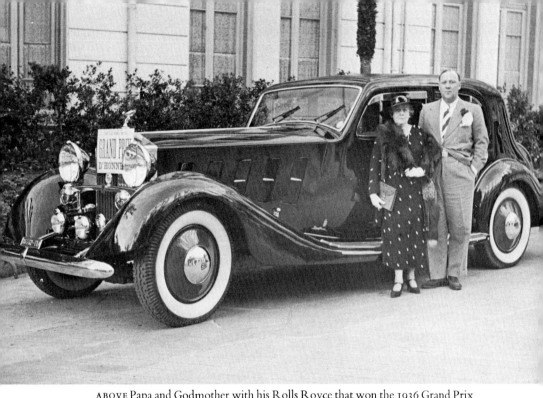

ABOVE Papa and Godmother with his Rolls Royce that won the 1936 Grand Prix d'Honneur in Monte Carlo

BELOW LEFT The chapel at Valsalice where the partisans hid their guns
BELOW RIGHT Orazio, my first love, as he looked in 1955

My confirmation

Me, grinning happily, in 1938

To Grannie
Love
Caterin
3/9/38

Richard and I outside the church in 1947

My first professional modelling job, in a Simone Mirman hat

How fashions and figures change!

A scene from *Dick Whittington* at Windsor; I'm standing on the steps

Learning to sing with Bertha Nicklass Kempner

to one side, it overlooks the softly undulating Tuscan hills on the other.

I found it very easy to study in this setting. I enjoyed looking up at the Pompeian frescoes on the walls, and watching gods gambolling across the ceilings of my classroom. The whole place was incredibly spacious; the wide corridors went on for miles, and from the huge classrooms with their high ceilings, steps led out of French windows onto the beautifully laid-out gardens, neat gravelled paths edging the well-kept lawns. Everything seemed to be sloping yet geometric.

Poggio was a Fascist-orientated school. Our headmistress, Signora (or Contessa, as many of the parents called her) Scopoli, was a rabid supporter of the regime and always addressed people by the official 'voi' instead of the softer, more traditional 'lei'. Apparently her predecessor had been reported to the Fascist authorities for refusing to allow Mussolini's speech to interrupt the normal meal schedule of the school, and had left soon afterwards. Signora Scopoli immediately had a radio installed in our dining-room so the question couldn't arise again. She also encouraged us to dress up in our uniforms of the Giovani Italiane (the Italian youth movement) and march proudly up and down the garden to the music of Fascist songs. Without realizing any of the political implications I thoroughly enjoyed these sessions. One of my particular favourites was the famous Fascist anthem 'Giovinezza' ('Youth'). Originally written in 1909 as a University of Turin song in praise of youth, it had been taken up by the Italian troops during the First World War. Later, different verses were written to it in honour of the Fascist Party but its original refrain and catchy tune made it quite different from other national anthems. It was composed by Maestro Guiseppe Blanc and I did not know then that his son, Orazio, was to become my very first beau and remain a close friend throughout my life.

Although I was at Poggio for only eighteen months, this school made a great impact on me, and some of the friends I made there still drift in and out of my life. One of them I knew as Blanca Rosa Welter; she was half-Mexican and half-Dutch and we all thought she was madly attractive. The two of us shared a love of dancing; in the evenings we used to set up gramophones blaring out the top pops of the time whilst we gave lessons to the more inhibited amongst us. She became well-known as actress Linda Christian and years later married Tyrone Power in a magnificent ceremony in Rome. He too became a good friend and was highly amused by my North Foreland childhood claims.

A string of celebrities came to Poggio either to present the prizes at the end of term or simply encourage us to study hard and well. These visits were always preceded by lots of extra spit-and-polish, and the floors became precariously slippery. On one such day, I came speeding along at a rate of knots, cut one of the corners too sharply and skidded to a halt at somebody's feet. I looked up at an imposing figure in a massive black cloak and a wide-brimmed hat. He carried a stick and tapped me gently as he looked down, smiled like a cherub and thanked me for my welcome. It was the great Maestro Pietro Mascagni, composer of *Cavalleria Rusticana*.

How ashamed I was, though, when my godmother, Princess Irene of Greece, came to present the end-of-term prizes. The only one I could hope for was for misconduct, but an honourable mention for embroidery, which I did get, somehow seemed even worse. Princess Irene came to Poggio as H.R.H. the Duchess of Spoleto and her husband had just been made King of Croatia – a role he was, in fact, never to play. It was a strange coincidence (my life seems to have been full of them) that at the school at the same time were the two daughters of the then Croatian President, and these two solid-looking Slavs were to become passively involved in my enforced departure from Poggio.

It happened at lunch one day while we were listening to the news. I'd never given much thought to politics as such. Of course I knew that Italy had now joined in the war and I was torn, in as much as I wanted both England and Italy to succeed and yet realized that this was impossible. Suddenly the announcer boomed out the news that Tobruk had fallen. I let out a whoop of joy – the silence around me was deafening, and all I could see opposite me were those two scowling Slavs. Without a second's hesitation I picked up my plate, piled high with Sunday lunch, and hurled it across the table. The sisters dodged and to my horror it was Signora Scopoli, passing by, who caught the full impact of the roast chicken and gravy.

From past experience I knew I had done it again. And this time, at the tender age of twelve, the reason for my departure was, of all things ... political.

Signora Scopoli, of whom I was very fond, called me in to her office. She was kind and not at all harsh, but she was soon joined by higher authorities, and with words like 'subversive influence', 'she has no pride in her name' and 'a disgrace to her father', I was shown to the door. I got into the Rolls and was driven back to Valsalice. The atmosphere at home was understandably sulphuric. I was genuinely penitent and, for the first time, in the depths of despair. I felt I had let everyone down and could quite well understand why I was left on my own for hours with only the dogs for company. I went all round the park, the vineyard, up into the woods, kicking stones and stumps of trees and thinking that this must be the end of the world. I remember shuffling into the chapel too, saying a prayer and then shuffling out again. I didn't know what else to do.

Eventually I learnt I was to be given one more chance. I was incredibly relieved and will always be grateful to my father for choosing to send me to the Collegio del Sacro Cuore in Rome. The convent stands attached to the Trinita dei Monti Church, right at the top of the Spanish Steps, and is one of the classic tourist views of Rome. From inside the building you look over the Piazza di Spagna, way across the city, to Castel Sant'Angelo and the dome of St Peter's.

My father accompanied me and we rang the bell. There was the sound of a lock being drawn and the clank of a chain, then a smiling sister pulled back the heavy oak door and welcomed us inside. By now I had become something of an expert on school atmospheres; here, as I stood in the incredible peace of the cloisters, I felt at last that I belonged. The Mother Superior, Mother de Thélin, greeted us with regal dignity, but warmth and understanding exuded through her sweet smile. The three of us spent a few minutes together, and then another mother joined us and we were shown briefly around the convent. So this was the start of another, happier chapter of my school life.

After the politically-slanted Poggio Imperiale I was immediately struck by the totally apolitical and gentler atmosphere of the Sacred Heart. There, one lived in a world apart. The nuns were on the whole very different from those at the Cabrini. I was aware of a hierarchy: there were the sisters who swept, cooked and generally looked after our physical needs; then there were the mothers with their different caps and veils. Most of these came from the aristocracy and, in that era, no pupil was admitted unless her family background was totally acceptable.

The nuns of the Sacred Heart had a tremendous influence on me. It was through them that I finally achieved a sense of self-discipline and a perspective on life without which I would have been totally lost. Three of the bywords of the Sacred Heart were cleanliness, health and modesty. For instance, we had regular baths but were always expected to wear our cotton shifts in the water. Curtains were drawn between the various tubs and the nun in charge would go along peeping through each one in turn to make sure that none of us had been so immodest as to appear before ourselves in the nude. Another weekly ritual was to have our hair fine-combed: cotton-wool was flaked and coaxed down between the teeth of a comb, which was then dragged along our scalps. Dandruff and dust may well have come forth but never, it was hoped, the dreaded lice. Then there was the garlic. A clove was crushed and wrapped in a dampened wafer. This we swallowed regularly to ward off colds and pimples. I cannot bear to think what we must have smelt like; nobody ever mentioned it, and we were certainly a very healthy lot. But one of the things I hated most on bitterly cold mornings was to have to crack a film of ice on my bedside bowl of water before I washed my face and cleaned my teeth at dawn. My neck, I confess, was left out on these mornings.

I can't pretend I was a paragon of virtue even at the Sacred Heart, but there was a compatibility between us – they seemed to understand my weaknesses. Many things stirred my emotions – not least a Jesuit priest (the Sacred Heart is the Sister Order to the Jesuits) who, to my eyes, was almost god-like. He led our retreats once a year: four days in which small groups at a time were set apart from the daily routine. We would listen to Father D'Aria talking; he would lead us into meditation and generally encourage us to revalue the spiritual side of life. I fell madly in love with him and my enthusiasm and motives for joining the group weren't as spiritually pure as they should have been. My heart literally missed a beat when I saw him; and I stumbled my way into the confessional just to hear him speak to me alone. By the time he blessed me I'd forgotten all my sins and just wanted him to keep talking. Maybe over the years we did become closer than we should have done, but it was only a strong undercurrent of affection. Maybe he enjoyed my liveliness and, fearing that I could become a lost sheep, wanted to keep me within the fold. All I do know is that we kept in close touch even after I came to England and I missed him deeply after his death, many years later, in Naples.

There was a spartan touch about the life at the Sacred Heart. Discipline was very rigid. I never quite got used to the six a.m. rising or going to daily Mass on an empty stomach. How I hated my badly and sometimes painfully flaking knees; but they were the inevitable result of all the hours we spent kneeling on hard wooden 'rests' through Mass, Benediction and Chapel sessions.

Mother Garnier, a small voluble French woman approaching seventy, with a tightly-wrinkled face and beady eyes, held us all in the palm of her hand. Amongst other things she led a class called '*Maintient*', which was virtually to instruct us in general behaviour.

'Although we have left the world we want you to go into it as gracefully as possible,' she said; so what we learnt was how to walk into a room. 'You are a presence, so carry yourself up straight. You appear, you do not scuttle in like a mouse.' On how to shake hands: 'Look into the eyes of the person you are greeting – you look shifty if you evade them.' On how to walk up and down stairs. 'Don't shuffle or slouch – walk tall.' And possibly my favourite: 'We don't cross our legs, but you are going to have to. Do so as gracefully as you can. Like this ...' The black-clad figure with the white-edged head-dress lifted her skirts, and the black-stockinged legs showed us just how. Looking at this class it too has paid useful dividends. It taught me to appear self-confident even when I am quaking inside, and by kidding others it helps me to kid myself that everything will be all right.

When I left the Poggio and went to the Sacred Heart I also switched horses scholastically. Leaving the Italian Magistrali system I joined the French stream, and aimed for a baccalaureate. It was obvious that I would not become a bluestocking so my father felt that I might as well increase my knowledge of French – after all this was a French convent.

Despite the war raging outside and the difficulties of travelling, there was more of a mixture of nationalities in *les classes Françaises*. One girl I remember vividly for her sense of humour and wicked sense of fun was Princess Josephine of the Belgians. The daughter of King Leopold and his beautiful queen, Astrid, who died tragically in a car accident, I imagine the Sacred Heart had been chosen for her so that she could be under the wing of her aunt, Crown Princess Maria José of Italy. Without the firm reins of discipline she would have been one of the worst kinds of practical jokers. As it was, she was limited to such things as smoking and blowing the smoke into my face so that I got the blame, and bending her knees into the backs of mine while going down stairs so I'd pitch forward with squeaks and squawks as we all collapsed like a pack of cards. Then again she'd take large flat rounds of transparent green peppermint (a delicious speciality of Doney's tea rooms in Florence) and shove one into my mouth just as I was about to be asked to go up to the blackboard. I longed to retaliate but, although we were told to call her Josephine, we were also expected to show a certain respect for H.R.H. Mixed in with usual high spirits there was a sadness in Princess Josephine – tears would often well up in her pale blue eyes; it was about that time that King Leopold was thinking of marrying the now Princess de Réthy.

A nun who influenced me tremendously was Mother Fusco, a fine woman, who was our headmistress. Her eyes shone gazelle-like out of a long pale face, so thin that from the side she was totally blinkered by her white pleated coif. Small and slim, she glided silently everywhere and gave the impression of being extremely austere until her fleeting, warm smile made her suddenly approachable. She must have suffered a great deal physically because throughout the winter her fingertips which peeped out from her woollen mittens were always puce, swollen and often raw. She established a most effective safety valve for any child who felt the need of one in the shape of a small chunky black notebook. Into this we would pour out our souls and leave our notes outside her office every evening. She must have stayed up to all hours of the night wading through the contents because, each morning, the booklet would be returned to our desk containing a comment from her on what we had written.

This was a time of my life when I badly needed to communicate with someone I felt would keep a secret. For once I had found in the Sacred Heart a place where I could settle down and do my best to behave well, and make amends for at least some of my misdemeanours at other schools. But I was very worried and sometimes frightened by what I thought might be going on at home. Although it was wartime I'd always received letters from Mama in Switzerland, so why had these stopped coming? Why did Papa avoid replying whenever I asked about her, and get crosser each time I asked again? Once he wrote and said, 'You mustn't be surprised, you know she never loved you.' All this dug deeply into my emotions. Then came the time when I got a curt letter from Papa to say that I wouldn't be going home for the next holidays because Godmother was feeling 'too tired to have me around'. Very upset about this I wrote to Godmother at once. No reply. So I sent another letter asking why. Only months later did I discover that she had never received them. I was beginning to feel rather insecure and lost; I knew it was not my behaviour this time. In Mother Fusco I found not only understanding but an astringent, constructive attitude. From her I began to learn self-reliance through a trust in God. I was a willing learner and kept scribbling away to her, which she must have found rather a problem – my writing was already illegible however I tried to change it.

It was while I was at the Sacred Heart that Orazio Blanc, the composer's son, came into my life to stay. We met at Bardonecchia, then a small resort in the Piedmont mountains.

'We all need some mountain air after spending the summer at Rapallo,' my father had said, so off we went, Godmother, Papa and myself. As usual I wasn't allowed to mix with the other children at the hotel, so I probably looked rather pathetic always tagging along with this odd couple, who looked more like mother and son than husband and wife. Days went by and all I dared do was exchange smiles with the youngsters as they left in a group for yet another outing in the glorious mountain sunshine.

We'd been there about a week when a slim, tanned young man, with bright blue eyes and a shock of blond hair, approached God-mother and asked, very politely, whether perhaps I couldn't join them all that evening as they were planning to go to a fairground nearby. This was Orazio, and after a good deal of persuasion Papa agreed, 'but only for an hour from eight till nine'. He made it sound like the most enormous favour. It certainly was a tremendous treat; what fun I had. The boys and girls were friendly and I had a go on everything: the roundabouts, the chutes, the shooting-range. Suddenly an hour and ten minutes had gone by and I broke out in a cold sweat. I had committed a major sin. Orazio and I left the others to continue their fun and rushed back, but we were nearly half an hour late when we reached the hotel. Papa was pacing up and down the hall looking thunderous. He glowered at his watch, dismissed Orazio, then pushed me up the stairs and into my room. 'Punctuality is the politeness of kings,' he said, and added a curt 'Goodnight' as he shut the door behind him.

I felt every inch a sinner but also thoroughly resentful. Why did I have to be singled out for what I considered to be ridiculous sever-ity? The next morning, when I joined Godmother and Papa in their suite for breakfast, the atmosphere was icy. I was told that it would be the last time I'd be allowed out in the evening, or for that matter at any time without them.

Orazio was not to be put off so easily. The day after, he approached the three of us on our morning walk. He apologized again and took the blame for being late back from the fair, then 'Would you object if Caterinella joined us for tennis this afternoon?' he asked, adding tactfully, 'you could come and watch if you wouldn't be too bored.' Maybe it was because when Papa was at school, at Fribourg in Swit-zerland, he had been a tennis champion and still enjoyed tennis of any kind, he relented and said yes. Off I went again under Orazio's protective wing. By now he was becoming my hero, and with an uncanny sense of prediction he even changed my name. Neither of us liked the Italian version of Catherine – Caterina – and agreed that Caterinella was too much of a mouthful, so he dubbed me 'Ketty'

– not so different from Katie but the important point at the time was that it made our combined initials O.K!

First love was in bud. Although never alone, we could occasionally link hands as we dropped back from the others walking through the mountain glens – and even though our first kiss was just a butterfly brush across the lips it was very romantic.

The day before we were due to leave, both Orazio and I were feeling predictably glum. Cocooned as I was by such obsessive severity it seemed unlikely that we would be able to stay in touch with each other. However, when we said goodbye that evening in front of a collection of parents and friends, Orazio slipped a note into my hand. It read 'see you later'. I couldn't think how as I was just going up to bed.

Sleep just wouldn't come and late into the night I was still gazing out of the window. All of a sudden I heard a rustle on the ground below. Within seconds Orazio had scaled up the uneven surface of the hotel wall and jumped through the window into my bedroom. His arms went round me. He crushed me to him as his lips found mine. For a few moments I gave no thoughts to Godmother and Papa a few rooms away. Then he shed his jacket, undid his shirt and slipped out of his trousers. I stood rooted to the floor until he gently led me to the bed. Gathering my nightdress tightly round me I followed him and, between the sheets, snuggled into his arms. He kissed my lips, my hair, my eyes but only ran his hands briefly over my body before clasping me to him again with infinite tenderness. We talked of love, of marriage, and it was then that we exchanged the vow of everlasting friendship which we have always kept.

He promised to write and send his letters to the Sacred Heart. He said that at half-term he would come to see me because he was going to tell my father that he loved me and that he would marry me when the war was over. He spoke of his determination to join the Alpini, the Italian Alpine troops; this he did with pride and recognized prowess (I still treasure the green and gold badge of his regiment). We talked until the black of the night turned to the slow glow of dawn. I was scared when I saw how light it had become, but he went safely, the way he'd come, leaving my very young heart bursting with emotion.

Orazio was as good as his word. When I returned to the Sacred Heart he wrote frequently, sent me telegrams and red roses, which according to a schoolmate, Maria Carmela Attolico (later Viscountess Hambledon), caused consternation amongst mothers and pupils alike. What is more, Orazio arranged to be in Rome at half-term and, over tea at the Ambasciatori Hotel, the ornate Mecca of respectable glamour in those days, he told my father that he loved me and hoped we would have his blessing on our marriage. This, I believe, was the only time in my life that I saw Papa nonplussed. Even he must have been taken aback by the frankness and obvious sincerity of this nineteen-year-old youth.

The explosion that Orazio and I expected never came. Papa just suggested logically that we should wait a while (I was almost fifteen by this time) and we parted starry-eyed, me to go back to the Sacred Heart, him to join his Alpine regiment. Unfortunately Papa put an immediate end to my receiving any more letters and although we managed to skirt round this veto whilst I was in Rome, it was impossible once I went home. Anyway events were taking a very strange turn back there and circumstances forced Orazio to fade into the background, at least for a few years.

A Family
in Italy

Valsalice is a green and hilly district on the outskirts of Turin which gave its name to our house. The villa itself had originally belonged to the Italian Royal Family. It was very attractive but always gave me the impression of a gem top-heavily mounted. The paths and drives seemed to go on for ever, as if the landscape artist couldn't quite decide when to stop. The sweeping lawns were, by contrast, decisive and impressive, often edged by life-size stone figures nestling in modestly-pruned ivy. A vineyard, which as far as I know never produced anything but rough cooking wine, flanked one of the hills, while thick woodland climbed to the top of another. This last was one of my favourite hiding-places as a child. From high up there I gazed often at the spectacular view which spanned the River Po and the whole of Turin. I felt protected and at peace with the world when I escaped from reality and sat on the moss at the foot of those trees.

We also had a small, neatly-domed chapel where Mass was said every Sunday and on feast days for ourselves and those who worked in the house or on the estate – some twenty or thirty people in all.

The entrance to Valsalice was up a wide, double staircase on to a marble-floored patio and then into the hall through an enormous pair of stained-glass doors depicting the spring and summer seasons. At the far end of the hall, opposite, there were two similar doors depicting autumn and winter. In turn these far doors opened on to an amphitheatre of lawns and rose gardens.

There were four huge pillars in the hall itself, the ceiling was ornate and at centre left stood a monumental 'walk in' chimney-piece, where a huge log-fire roared behind wrought-iron gates as soon as there was a sign of winter. A staircase led, with a sweeping sense of superiority, from this hall to the *galleria* on the first floor. How I enjoyed these stairs – they were low, wide ones, which I could scale at least two at a time, edged with perfect 'slide down' banisters – if you didn't get caught!

The *galleria*, as it suggests, was a picture gallery; the walls were filled with paintings of every description from the Italian Primitives to the French Impressionists. A Salvador Dali even looked down on us for a while. Every table-top seemed to be crammed with treasures as well. I was probably over-conscious of them because we always had afternoon tea either in the *galleria* or on its terrace, and I only had to wriggle slightly for someone to shout, 'Careful! Don't knock anything over!' Of course I resented this at the time, but I suppose it did teach me to be more thoughtful than most children at that awkward age. I have to admit that this early training paid dividends as I grew up.

A vast ballroom led off the *galleria* and that first floor also included an impressively sombre library, a rambling two-bedroom suite with a couple of bathrooms, which Godmother and Papa shared, and two large terraces, like arms outstretched, on either side of the house.

I always felt that the architect must have altered his original plan, because the only way to the second floor was up a narrow spiral staircase. Even the carpet on it was coarse and different. These stairs ran from the kitchens, which were well below ground level, right up to the top of the house, where there was a maze of corridors and bedrooms.

I always felt ill-at-ease on these stairs and it was there that I met my first ghost. She didn't scare me in the least. It was mid-afternoon and I was running up to my bedroom to change after playing tennis when I had to stop to let a figure, all in white, go by. The thought did flash through my mind that it was a bit early in the day for someone to be wearing an evening dress but as I had met a few unusual people already I didn't take too much notice. I remember saying, 'Good afternoon.' She replied with the most beautiful smile and at the same time offered me an apple from the basket she was carrying. I can still hear my reply: 'No thank you very much, I'm so thirsty I need a glass of water more than anything else,' then I flew on up the stairs.

On the next bend I glanced down automatically. There was no sign of anyone at all. Although I wasn't afraid, I felt that the individual I had spoken to had nothing whatsoever to do with this world. She was in fact the White Lady whom so many people coming to Valsalice had seen wafting through the hedges and bushes near the tennis court, especially on moonlit nights; there were all kinds of stories about her. Later, I told Godmother of my experience. 'Really,' she said, 'the only thing that worries me is that when she is seen indoors it is supposed to mean that great unhappiness will come to the house and family.' At that moment I had an odd and very strong feeling that this would be so.

I'd never liked that spiral staircase but now I became scared of it. It didn't help either that the walls were laden with austere Piranesi prison prints, and from that day I always ran both up and down those stairs, looking back over my shoulders in case some cruel warden would dart out from a frame and catch me. We always seem to attract the very dangers we fear most. Maybe I did just this, because in years to come this house with its spiral staircase was to become a prison for me.

The ballroom with its giant crystal chandeliers, domed ceiling and candle brackets round the walls, was a focal point of Valsalice. By the French windows were two pianos and a harp, and when Godmother and Papa were first married they had many musical evenings in that room. Well-known pianists, harpists and singers were invited to perform, and on such evenings I used to peep through a door and watch as the guests arrived, shed their magnificent coats, cloaks and furs in the hall, then flowed up the stairs in full and sparkling regalia. Occasionally I was allowed to put on my first long evening dress (predictably made of pale blue taffeta) and join the crowd. How I hated having to go to bed early after making the *de rigueur* curtsey to everyone.

Godmother played both the piano and the harp. She had a sweet singing voice too and set many words, especially French verses, to

music. My favourite is still an anonymous 'recipe' for a happy marriage. The original, written in illuminated lettering on pale yellow
wood, has hung in every home I have had. In English it reads like
this:

> To begin with put into a bowl
> Two or three pounds of hope,
> Then you add a ton
> Of caring and understanding.
> Now comes a measure of kindness and
> A hundredweight of trust.
> Put what you will of gaiety,
> And four or five pots of obedience,
> To blend with five or six pounds of sweetness.
> There's no need whatsoever for monotony
> And be sure you add to good humour
> Just a dash of madness.
> As for salt, not more than one grain
> Because if you have more of this,
> Instead of an ounce, you'll have to put at least two of patience.
> Now simmer the mixture at a well-sustained heat,
> And never lose sight of either love or friendship.
> By doing all this you will have cooked a well-balanced pie,
> A slice of which each morning
> Will be enough to embellish your life

My father also sang; his voice and Godmother's blended beautifully. He had the soft voice of a diseur and all the lights and shades
of a born entertainer. Old English love songs, Italian and Neapolitan
ballads, Russian folk songs, French cabaret numbers and American
negro spirituals were all in his repertoire, and I could be moved to
tears by many of them.

On one of my school holidays I came home to find a little corner
of Tzarist Russia had been established at Valsalice. Italy having joined
in the war, Genoa became an obvious target for enemy aircraft, so
Papa and Godmother persuaded Nonna to shut up her flat there and
gave her a ground-floor wing of Valsalice. With her came her sister,
Nadine, and Nadine's daughter Lily. These two were tragic refugees
from the Russian revolution. Nadine Oboukhoff, the widow of the

Director of the Bolshoi Theatre in Moscow, after some horrific experiences at the start of the Revolution, had managed to get on to a train to France with her daughter Lily, her son-in-law and twelve-year-old grandson Nicholas; but just as they were moving out of the station Lily's husband was torn from the train never to be seen or heard of again. They eventually reached Paris, where they scraped together a miserable existence selling matches and shoelaces on street-corners, and doing any menial jobs they could find.

In the meantime Nicholas was growing up and, probably due only to his efforts to provide a better life for his mother and grandmother, got himself into serious money trouble. My father came to his rescue in as much as Godmother paid off his debts and he was shipped off to the Foreign Legion whilst Nadine and Lily were brought to Italy to live with Nonna.

Nonna and Tante Nadine, as I called her, lived until they were well into their nineties and must have been approaching eighty when they came to stay with us. Despite the generation gap, Lily did not look that much younger: all the emotional traumas she had been through had taken a cruel toll on her physically – six feet tall, she stooped slightly and was painfully thin; her bright beady eyes had sunk deep into her bony face. Tante Nadine, even though her face was parchment-dry and tightly wrinkled, still bore the traces of having been a great beauty; her features were small, her translucent blue eyes large, and her whole face lit up into a glorious smile. There was an incredible softness and warmth about her. Nonna could never have been pretty – her chin was too long, her eyes too small – but with her upright carriage and general air of determination she was a strong personality.

I loved all three of them dearly and would often listen open-mouthed as each one followed her own line of thought. Nonna (more of a *gourmande* than a *gourmet*) would begin: 'Nadine, I think we will have chicken and rice for dinner. *Ach* [a typically Russian sound], that will be delicious!' Nadine followed on with, 'Katia, my dear, do you remember the first ball we went to at the Palace? You were dressed in blue – I chose yellow and had lots of green leaves all over my crinoline. The Tzar danced with me and told me how pretty I was...' By now her eyes were filled with tears. Lily, meanwhile, poring over an outspread map on the other side of the room, stated categorically, 'It is quite impossible. The Germans cannot win the war.'

How many happy hours I spent with them. Their part of the house became a refuge for me when sparks were flying elsewhere. A focal point for me was a wall in Nonna's bedroom where she hung a jewelled icon of the black Madonna and Child of Kazan which had been given to her by the Tzarina. Just underneath the icon a candle burnt in a red glass container which was suspended on a gold chain, and there was a bowl of flowers on the table below. This icon now hangs in my own bedroom and reminds me daily of three very dear Russian ladies.

We spoke French together, but they always spoke Russian to each other and it has been one of my great regrets that I should have let such a chance to speak that language slip by. I can't think why I did, because it was there to be absorbed with only the slightest effort. I did the same thing over learning to play the piano – I simply refused. How short-sighted one can be when one is young.

Tante Nadine and Lily were of course deeply grateful to God-mother and Papa for changing their lives so completely, but I always felt that they were just a little scared of my father, even Nonna tensed when he was around. It didn't help that, in his soft-soled shoes, he'd often appear without warning. Unless he was in a very good mood these three old ladies seemed to irritate him, and the more they chattered in welcome the more impatient I felt him become.

It was their mania for squirrelling food in their cupboards which really drove him mad. Although Nonna didn't share the gruesome memories of Tante Nadine and Lily of having to eat rats and rotten potatoes in Russia to stave off the pangs of hunger, she was the worst offender. Little paper packets of cheese, biscuits, fruit, chocolate, half-finished jars of jam and honey – they all found their way to one special cubby-hole. Papa could sniff out the faintest smell and was always on the look-out for crumbs. As a rule he would growl a bit and entreat them to have their maid, Adelina, bring whatever they wanted from the kitchen, but their instinct for self-preservation was far too strong for them and it was not long before they'd start to hoard again.

One terrible morning Papa stormed in looking for trouble. You could have cut the atmosphere with a knife when he suddenly opened that cupboard. With a roar of rage and a sweep of his hand he sent all the treasures flying across the room. 'I forbid you to turn this place ino a pigsty,' he bellowed. 'Either you stop this filthy habit, or you'll have to go!' With that he stormed out ... and we were left surveying the sticky wreckage!

My father was such a complex, paradoxical character that I find it very difficult to analyse my feelings towards him. He was over-kind one moment, downright cruel the next, unreasonably strict, then ludicrously lenient. Amoral himself, he was intolerant of immorality in others. I'm quite sure he would have wanted me to remain a virgin forever; yet, when I was still in my early teens, he would call me to his bed where I would cuddle up to him and together we would pore over an outsize sex encyclopedia, which he would explain in detail and at great length. But wherever and whatever, he was always larger than life.

As a child I worshipped him. I always wanted to be in his arms, and he was just as prepared to hold me. His quick flashes of irritability did not touch me at all. Later, when he justifiably flared up against my naughtiness, I couldn't rest until I had re-established our physic-ally affectionate relationship. Once he'd hugged me, I felt everything was all right again. Gradually, as I began to acquire the faculty to reason, I felt fear when I watched him explode over some triviality. I worried because at times he appeared grossly unfair.

It all happened so suddenly. I was at Valsalice. Our doctor arrived with another man, whom he introduced to Papa as Professor Stropeni, then all three of them went upstairs to Godmother's bedroom. After what seemed to me a very long time they came out again. They looked grave. In the hall the Professor shook hands with my father. 'I assure you, Marchese, the sooner I operate the better. I'll go to the hospital immediately and make the necessary arrangements.'

'How very kind of you. I know my wife is in the best of hands.'

My heart froze and when the car left I ran to Papa. 'Is Godmother ill?'

'Yes, she has to have a very serious operation.'

I didn't dare ask anything more, so I just held his hand until he left me outside her door.

Nobody had time for me. I watched as the maid packed a small suitcase and went downstairs to hand it to the chauffeur who'd brought the car round to the front door. Soon afterwards God-mother came down with Papa. He had his arm round her protec-tively. I ran to her and she held me very tightly. 'Be good, little one, won't you.' Then they were gone. It's incredible how that large house, full of servants and dogs, suddenly became so empty when this small elderly woman left. No smiles, no chattering, certainly no laughter, and when my father came back late that night, he looked tired and drawn.

The days that followed the operation were very worrying and I was only allowed to see Godmother once at the Sanatrix nursing home. The room was softly-lit and she looked frail, her white hair and pale face accentuated by the pink bedclothes. I hardly dared to touch the small hand she held out towards me.

'Gently,' murmured Papa. He must have felt that I wanted to throw myself onto the small figure and sob with relief to see her alive. I'd been so very frightened ever since she had been taken away and nobody would tell me what was really happening.

One day, when she was still in hospital, Papa and I were having tea in the library.

Papa looked very sad as he gazed into the flames of the fire, so I went over and sat on the floor beside him. He stroked my hair and said, 'You know, don't you, Caterinella, that Godmother has been very seriously ill.'

I nodded and he went on. 'The surgeon has had to cut off one of her breasts.'

'Why?' I could hardly whisper.

'So as to stop something called a cancer from spreading all through her body and killing her.' The silence was loud between us.

'She won't die now though, will she?'

'No, the surgeon thinks he has caught things in time,' he replied. 'Breasts are a very important part of a woman's body – especially when a man and woman love each other. Remember what I'm say-ing now, and when you grow up you'll understand.'

Many months later I was sitting in the bathroom while Godmother lay back and soaked in the warm water. The scar across
her breast was a long one and reached right under her arm, but by
now it had lost its redness. My eyes were drawn to it – Godmother
glanced down too and ran a finger along the neat embroidery. When
she looked up her expression was infinitely sad. 'The surgeon said
it was such a pity to cut off such a beautiful breast.'

She must have been getting on for seventy and her remaining
breast was still firm and round. At that moment I felt I was already
beginning to understand what my father had been talking about;
what I couldn't have imagined was the added anguish to a woman
so much older than her husband.

At that stage though I easily pushed such thoughts aside. I was
only too happy to share my love of Papa with Godmother. I treasure
memories of the three of us just being loving and happy together:
climbing to the Sanctuary of Montallegro above Rapallo – horribly
commercialized now, but then just a small huddle of houses on the
way up to the church – where we would eat delicious lasagne verdi,
then walk in the woods with the dogs and perhaps stay the night
in the spartanly-bare but spotlessly-clean rooms overlooking the
Tigullio Bay far below.

Nobody could have been better company than Papa when he was
in a good mood and I don't think I am the only one who thought
he could charm the birds out of the trees. As time went by, though,
I became aware of his other characteristics. His inability to keep
friends he made – he attracted people like a magnet and would
be the pivot of any party. I have seen both men and women spell-
bound in his presence, and there is no one word that conveys the
effect he had on them. Perhaps it was the combination of his warmth,
humour, charm and superb manners which made each individual
feel that he or she was the only one who really mattered. His attitude
towards paying certain bills was somewhat unconventional: he
would be astounded, slightly hurt in fact, that anyone would con-
sider doing such a thing as charging for the privilege of giving him
advice. He was in fact beginning to show signs of megalomania.

After spending the winter months at Valsalice, Godmother and
Papa would set off in the late spring, for Rapallo, where from June

to September they lived in the Villa Delmitia. The exodus usually meant that Papa drove Godmother and me, plus four of the favourite pekes, in the open Dilambda, whilst Filiberto, the chauffeur, followed in the Rolls, complete with a couple of maids, the head butler and the rest of the livestock – two Siamese cats in baskets, a large cage of budgies, a smaller one with a canary and further assorted dogs. We always left at dawn so as to be there before the heat of the day, with everyone in holiday mood and with me well-dosed with homeopathic pills to stop me being sick on the mountain bends.

Villa Delmitia nestled into the hill above the road between Rapallo and San Michele; we only had to cross over the road to reach the gardens which led steeply down to the sea and our own jetty. From the Kursaal, which formed part of the Hotel Excelsior, I could see lots of people diving into the water and scrambling on and off the rocks. How I wished I could join them, but then it's very difficult to appreciate the luxury of privacy when you're very young.

I spent most of my days in and out of the water and was taught to swim by our boatman. He simply chucked me into the sea way out of my depth and watched me dog-paddle for survival. It was he who looked after our small dinghy, the *Patino*, and the glorified sailing-boat. On this we sped along the coast as far as Portofino and San Fruttuoso – I can still smell the delicious fresh seafood feasts we had on the beach.

We saw locals such as Oskar Kokoschka the painter who, with his colourful style, was to find fame in the United States after the war, and Ezra Pound, the American poet, with his subdued wife who occasionally came to the Villa but were always to be seen walking together around Rapallo.

I can't remember exactly how and when Augusta came into my life but during one of my summer holidays at Rapallo, I gradually became aware that she was there. She was the daughter of a local postman; small and dark, beautifully voluptuous, with a shining mane of copper-coloured hair, strong white teeth and sparkling eyes, she glowed with health and vitality. She was also naturally friendly, often bringing flowers for Godmother and little presents for me.

Papa laughed a lot when Augusta was about. She was only twelve years older than me and, therefore, a great deal younger than Godmother, who generously showed no resentment at all; this may have been in part because Augusta appeared to be well in with a great many individuals of authority – I've certainly always felt that her feminine approach did a lot to protect my father from what could have been the fatal consequences of his political wheelings and dealings. What I didn't realize at the time was the important role she was going to play in my life.

War and
All That

As far as I was concerned things didn't change much even after Italy declared war. I connected nothing evil with the silver-grey ships that anchored from time to time just off the coast, any more than with the German naval officers who came to swim or lunch or dine with us. They often wore civilian clothes, were young and good-looking, and Godmother and Papa always remarked on their exceptionally good manners.

On the other hand, workmen were building a high wall of reinforced concrete along the sea front. I asked why and they told me, 'It's to make sure that the enemy can't land here.' Curfew was observed religiously and of course not a sliver of light could be seen from the house after dark.

Godmother often looked worried – she had heard nothing from her relations in England, and when we listened to the BBC news, Papa would throw a blanket over the radio to muffle the faintest sound – not even the servants who'd been with the family for years knew that we were listening.

One morning Papa came in with a handful of forms and passed them to Godmother. 'This is quite ridiculous,' he said, 'we have to fill these in to prove we haven't any Jewish blood for at least a couple of generations back.'

'And if we have, what happens?' she asked.

'Well, apparently Mussolini has agreed to Hitler's request that Italian Jews must be sent off to Germany and be put in work-camps too.'

Although my father was full of prejudices, he himself violently resented other peoples', and his pro-Jewish feelings dated back many years. Apparently, when he was still a young man in Florence, he overheard that later one evening a group of Fascists planned to rough up one of his Jewish friends at his home for no reason other than that he was a Jew. Papa immediately jumped on his motorbike, arrived at Via la Marmora and announced to a somewhat surprised Baron Zeggio that he was staying for dinner. Predictably, when the Fascists arrived a few hours later, their plan was deflated by the sight of the Vice Federale dining with their would-be victim.

It wasn't surprising therefore that after having filled in our forms that morning in Rapallo proving our Aryan stock, Papa set out to do what he could to prevent any Jewish friends of ours being taken away. There was one friend in particular he tried to help – a young concert pianist, Renato Cohen. He had suffered from polio when he was a child and still limped badly and he'd been on the threshold of international fame when war broke out. Instead he'd had to settle for playing to small, though appreciative, audiences around the Liguria, but more frequently he performed at Nazi functions for which, just because he was a Jew, he never got paid.

One morning the news came that a large truck had been seen stopping at various Jewish homes along the Riviera the night before; men, women and children had been dragged out, then pushed into it. Renato had been one of them. Everyone was saddened and I had rarely seen my father more upset, but the full horror of this incident came many months later when Renato's remains were returned anonymously to a friend of his – in the form of a lampshade.

Not long after Godmother had come back from hospital, Papa decided that there must be a Thanksgiving Mass in the chapel to celebrate. 'And', he announced, 'it will be to music.' He seemed to have no idea of how this would be done. The only source of music was the radiogram in the ballroom, which was half a house and a long terrace away from the Chapel. But Papa was right, this was just a detail. The day following this decision, a small convoy of vans beetled up the drive and a dozen or so busy men poured out. They off-loaded miles of wiring and masses of electrical gadgetries. They scurried about, chattering twenty to the dozen (nineteen was far too slow), and didn't leave until Gounod's '*Ave Maria*' was soaring forth from the chapel. Two days later another two vans came up the drive and made straight for the side of the chapel; I thought the same men were back again so I went to see what they were doing. But something made me stop behind a tree. Out came four men. They were bearded, roughly-dressed, wore heavy boots and seemed to be in a great hurry. They looked around furtively. 'Get a move on – but go carefully,' I heard one say.

Then they began to off-load guns! Not only guns of all shapes and sizes, but masses of ammunition too – and it was all being pushed into the chapel. In less than no time they had stacked the lot; there was so much of it that it reached to the top of a large painting behind the altar.

I held my breath. I suddenly realized – these men were partisans: anti-Fascist and anti-German soldiers who hid in the mountains in the north of Italy. They collected arms and helped escaped POWs whilst waiting to join up with the Allies as they advanced. The fact that they were bringing weapons closer to the city could only mean that civil war was in the air. I was scared stiff, though I had no idea how closely involved I would be when it eventually happened. At that particular moment, all I wanted to do was run away.

On Sunday morning, as the chapel bells were ringing, a car-load of German officers arrived. Papa had invited them for lunch, but as they were Catholics they also wanted to attend Mass. Later, when we sat down, I looked at these Nazis across the table and wondered what would happen to us if they knew that they had been only a painting away from all that enemy ammunition. What neither they nor I would have dreamed was that far below the dining-room, in the corner of the wine cellar, Papa was also sheltering a British prisoner of war.

This juggling of loyalties summed up my father's attitude to the war. Whatever the outcome he could, in all sincerity, claim to have been of assistance to the winner. To this end he also took great care to choose influential individuals in each camp who would be able to vouch for him later. Franco Damone was one of them. To all appearances he was a major of the *carabinieri*, the Italian Police Force; in fact he was also an important member of the Secret Police.

Needless to say I was totally unaware of this until very much later. He was in his late thirties when he came into my life. Six feet tall, slim, with dark hair greying at the temples, he moved with the grace of a tiger and his broad jaw-line and deep-set eyes beneath bushy brows were softened by a wide mouth which smiled easily.

Papa, as was his wont with new acquaintances, made an exaggerated fuss of Major Damone, inviting him to Valsalice almost every other day. Godmother liked him too but found it a bit wearing having to entertain his wife and six children as well. To be fair, Signora Damone probably felt just as embarrassed by such overpowering hospitality, because she and the children appeared less and less on the scene. I was rather sorry about this because I enjoyed their company. Anyway, minus his family Franco became more a part of ours. He and Papa would spend hours closeted in the library; they would go for long walks together locked in earnest conversation. Godmother and I soon took it for granted that he'd turn up unexpectedly for meals and even when we left Valsalice to spend the summer months at Rapallo, Franco would often be there too.

In June 1940 it was announced that Mussolini would address the nation. The three of us sat in the ballroom, a semi-circle of servants standing behind us, as Mussolini's voice boomed out of the radio-gram. He spoke of his pride in Italy for joining Hitler's Germany in the war against Great Britain. Godmother shuddered and as Papa put his arm protectively round her, she sobbed against his shoulder. All I can remember thinking was: Where is my mother?

On the very first night that Italy joined the war, we heard the drone of planes approaching Turin and stepped out onto the balcony. The view over the city was magnificent. Searchlights slashed the sky, and in their beams the British planes showed up silver. Then there came the thud of bombs, followed by spectacular explosions. The effect was totally unreal; we felt strangely uninvolved and completely unaware of the danger – until suddenly there was a loud whistle, then an almighty crash as shrapnel shaved off a corner of the balcony on which we were standing. We stepped back, stunned ... and finally realized that we were at war.

It must have been the middle of the night some years later, when we were all well into the war, that my bedroom door suddenly crashed open and all the lights snapped on. Augusta appeared, accompanied by a couple of uniformed Fascists. Her hair was tousled, she looked scared and had obviously been dragged out of bed. I jumped up and grabbed my dressing-gown, while the two soldiers pulled the curtains back roughly as though they were looking for somebody. Finding no one they shoved both of us along the corridor and down the stairs into the main hall. There we found Nonna, Tante Nadine and Lily huddled together, their faces as white as sheets, with armed soldiers standing over them. Papa was engaged in earnest conversation with another Fascist.

'If you will let me telephone Major Damone he will clear up the whole thing immediately. This accusation is absolutely ridiculous,' he said. Augusta and I looked at each other.

'You'll make no telephone calls,' barked the officer.

'We'll go out together – I want to see for myself.' My father looked straight ahead as they went down the front stairs; the Fascist was brandishing an out-sized torch.

By now the whole household was in uproar; the dogs were making a terrible racket and the servants, ashen-faced and clutching their nightclothes about them, were being prodded into the hall at gunpoint. None of us had the slightest idea what was going on, but we realized that we were in great danger. It seemed forever before the door leading on to the back lawns opened and the two men came back. My father was saying, 'I told you, my friend, that you would find nothing. But now I insist that you telephone.' His whole attitude had changed.

'I'll put the call through to the Major myself,' said the officer.

This time they went up the main stairs. Still surrounded by these armed soldiers none of us dared move – it looked as though it wouldn't have taken much for them to touch a trigger. The minutes ticked by. Finally Papa and the officer came back. The two exchanged Fascist salutes, the officer called the soldiers away and bade my father a curt 'Goodnight'. We breathed again only when the sound of their boots had faded and the cars were well away down the drive.

Apparently what had happened was that an anonymous telephone call had been put through to the Fascist headquarters and they had acted immediately on the information that my father was harbouring a British POW in the villa. There's no doubt whatsoever that by taking full responsibility for my father, and persuading the Fascist officer that there was no likelihood that Papa was collaborating with the enemy, Franco Damone certainly saved my father's life that night and possibly ours as well.

My feelings towards Franco were muddled – I suppose as any early teenager's might be towards any older man – and I certainly felt a strong physical attraction for him. Guilt played no part whatsoever in this, though I still saw his family from time to time. Now, instead of running to him with a hug as if he were a favourite uncle when he appeared, I felt pleasantly self-conscious. Another thing that endeared him to me was that he was very fond of Godmother and I knew she liked and trusted him too. Also, we regarded him as a buffer as Papa's outbursts got more frequent.

One day Godmother asked me straight out, 'Do you find Damone attractive?'

I had never lied to her. 'Well, I feel different when he's here.'

I certainly had an overwhelming desire to touch him and to be touched. It happened fleetingly at first: he'd rest a hand lightly on my shoulder – I would brush past him in a doorway – our eyes would meet and linger that fraction too long. Then suddenly, from one day to the next, I felt he was avoiding me completely. With the ruthlessness, or maybe just the thoughtlessness of youth, it never occurred to me that he might be fighting an inner turmoil. I just knew that what I was feeling was wonderful, and was desperately upset that it might stop.

It was at this time that I felt the atmosphere at Valsalice had changed. There was an undercurrent of tension which spread over the house and it seemed to affect everyone. The servants, who would usually go on chattering if I went into the ironing-room when they were sorting the linen or doing the mending, would suddenly fall silent when I appeared. If the butler came out of the dining-room and saw my father in the hall, he'd step back and quietly pull the door to. The respect that Papa might have commanded to begin with was definitely turning to fear. It was now an everyday occurrence to hear my father shouting. Rather than listen I used to run away, but the tirades coming through the closed doors were directed at Godmother. I heard money mentioned: 'Well, if you don't think I can be trusted I don't want to know.' Then it was her friends: 'I forbid him to come to this house again.'

And it was a fact that, one by one, Godmother's friends did stop coming to see her both at Valsalice and the Villa Delmitia. Even the most devoted ones telephoned more rarely. I never heard God-mother's voice raised in anger, but I noticed that her eyes were often red-rimmed, and they'd fill with tears when I reached out for her hand. Her smile, too, was wistful.

Our relationship became even closer, but whereas Papa encouraged this when they were first together, he now appeared to resent us being happy in each other's company; and when I asked Godmother what was wrong she'd reply: 'Nothing darling, nothing at all,' and keep her eye apprehensively on the door.

Then there was the ludicrous incident of the pear tree. Papa was convinced that Giovanni Grande (a giant of a gardener, hence the name, and as honest as the day is long) was going to 'steal' the last pear on it. Instead of simply picking it for himself, my father sat for hours behind a curtained window watching the tree and nursing a shotgun. When the pear eventually fell, rotten, to the ground, he was bitterly disappointed. In turn other members of the staff, to whom he'd always previously been affable, became a target for his growing persecution mania, and as for me, I could do nothing right.

Godmother's cough was a short, hard, persistent one but she made little of it and nobody attributed much importance to it. She began to complain of feeling more tired than usual – her siestas lasted longer and she got up later in the mornings. Then Papa received the results of some x-rays, and a few days after I overheard him telling Franco that the cancer had spread to her lung. 'It's only a matter of time now,' were his words.

I froze, but my brain raced round in panic. This could only mean that Godmother would die. I wanted to run to her and implore her not to leave me. Luckily, something stopped me because, at that stage, she still knew nothing of her death sentence.

My father seemed to react to the news in different ways at the same time. He certainly put his arm round her often in public, told her he loved her and made sure that her every whim and physical comfort were attended to immediately; but the dreadful shouting still came from their quarters and at meal-times the tension was so great that Godmother, the three old Russian ladies and I would eat in silence rather than risk his wrath for some triviality. We were not always that successful because once he threw a large bowl of spaghetti across the table. It missed me, but made a mess on the carpet and furniture.

One afternoon I went into the library to find Godmother at her desk. She held a pen in her hand above a half-written letter. Papa stood over her. Obviously neither of them heard me. I stood very still. Papa's expression was so set and hard, a chill went down my spine: 'Well, go on. You know exactly what you have to write.'

His fist was clenched and for one moment I thought he was about to hit her. Her face was frighteningly pale.

'You have no choice, Delphine. You know that, don't you!' His hand went to the back of her neck and I saw the knuckles whiten.

'But I must take care of my nieces, Mitia.' It was a plea.

'Don't you worry about them,' he retorted. 'You do what I tell you now!'

She looked so small and helpless. Suddenly, with all my strength, I hurled myself at him. I punched, kicked, bit and screamed abuse in an attempt to protect Godmother from I did not quite know what. But my father was a strong man and it didn't take him long to get this battling banshee under control and, as soon as I could break away, I flew to my room sobbing uncontrollably. Nothing was said to me about the incident, but, added to everything else, it made me realize that something very sinister was going on around me.

I felt desperately vulnerable and alone. There was no news from my mother. I did know by this time that she was living in Switzerland and that she had a new husband, Giacinto Scelsi, but Papa brushed aside any questions I asked about her and made me feel that she was uninterested in me.

By now our circle of friends and acquaintances had dwindled so much there was only Franco to turn to. I told him about the incident in the library; he listened quietly and then said something about my father having a lot to worry him.

The months that followed became a nightmare and I gradually realized that we were being cut off from the rest of the world. Papa took complete charge of all incoming and outgoing mail, and even sacked one maid on the spot when he found the poor woman had a letter to post for Godmother. Other servants who had been in the household for years were intimidated, and a number of them left.

We were never allowed to answer the telephone and if we tried to make a call we would hear an extension being picked up. He would behave as though he were trying to catch us out talking about him or 'plotting' against him. He also made quite certain that Godmother, Franco and I could never be alone together – he was always present.

Above all he seemed to be determined that Godmother should have no contact whatsoever with her solicitor. Each time my own resentment built up and overcame my fear, I made pathetic attempts to take him on. At other times I'd try in vain to reason with him. I asked so often what this virtual 'imprisonment' was all about. His reply was always the same: 'I'm protecting you all. The political situation outside is very grave.'

But nothing about this reign of terror made any sense until one day Godmother explained that on the day I'd fought with my father in the library, he had forced her to alter her will. Suddenly I understood that on top of all his other fears the recurrence of Godmother's illness had brought him the added one that she might not leave him everything she had. The surgeon had already told Papa that another operation could do nothing to help Godmother's condition so, apart from Franco, the only outsider to visit us was the doctor.

My hopes soared when one day he suggested a little sea air might make Godmother feel better. We packed and set off for Rapallo, but there was neither an improvement in her health nor a change in our personal freedom. When we first arrived there Godmother wrote to her solicitor and I said I'd slip out and post it; unfortunately I did not have the key to get back through the gate and she was afraid I might be caught anyway, so she tore up the note. Papa's secretary came to stay overnight but he made sure that Godmother did not see him alone. Franco occasionally came over from Turin and we were thrilled to see him. Apart from him and the Dottoressa Bacigalupo, our charming woman doctor who'd been a friend for years, we had no other visitors.

It was late evening on 3 February 1944. I had been watching Godmother as she slept. Every now and then she'd groan softly and I'd stroke her hand; it was soft and very dry. Her breathing was shallow and irregular. I prayed so hard that it wouldn't stop. Her eyes were sunken deep into their sockets and the bridge of her nose was stained dark. Maria, her devoted old maid, waddled in and replaced the jug of water. She looked at Godmother and then glanced at me and I could see that she had been crying. I wished she'd stay, then was glad she didn't. Although I'd never seen death before I felt it was very close indeed. There was no fear in me; instead, there was anguish – deep down inside as though someone was crushing everything there was of me. A tight band gripped my throat and I wanted to cry out, but no sound came. Tears burnt hot behind my eyes. This was Godmother – the woman who'd been my world ever since I could remember, and I knew I was losing her forever. As if she heard my thoughts, she turned her head. Her blue eyes opened wide and she smiled at me. I leant towards her but as I did her cheek dropped heavily on to the pillow – she was dead.

Franco came over from Turin immediately and I felt less lost the moment he arrived. I had never thought of all the practical things that have to be done when somebody dies, and just watched in a daze as people kept coming and going from Godmother's room. Papa decided that everyone on the estate might like to come and pay their last respects, so she was embalmed.

The curtains were drawn and the large candles lit at the four corners of the big double bed where she died gave the room a warm glow. The bedclothes and cream lace cover were unnaturally smooth and Godmother looked tiny as she lay there. Her face, softly framed in pink chiffon, bore the shadow of a smile and I thought she looked happy again. Was she perhaps next to me, looking at herself, I wondered? Huddled in a dark corner, I watched as people came to her bedside. Some knelt, some just stood with bowed head for a few moments, and lots of them were crying unashamedly as they left.

A Prisoner
at Home

We went back to Valsalice after the funeral; the house felt even larger and emptier now. How Papa felt I really cannot say. He was an emotional man who could cry easily and I did see him cry during the first few weeks. But, most of the time, I remember him talking for hours on the telephone behind closed doors. If I went in he would shoo me away.

I was seventeen and had left school by now but was not allowed to go into Turin on my own and there really wasn't anyone to take me. I often took refuge in Nonna's wing of the house. Tante Nadine, Lily and she were very subdued, and desperately worried now that Godmother was gone. Papa's extreme changes of mood made them feel insecure.

'Do you think he'll want us to leave?' they used to ask each other. But where could they go? Nonna's flat in Genoa had been returned to the landlord, and her other children in Florence were certainly not equipped to welcome the three of them. Papa did in fact keep them with him until many years later when, one by one, they died.

When Godmother died, the bottom fell out of my world. Without her my fear of Papa grew, and with it I found an added resentment towards him. The days dragged by. I spent hours on my filmstar albums. For as long as I can remember I had collected movie magazines and cut out pictures and stuck them in with loving care. I really treasured this collection and never more than now did I need this escape from reality into its pages. As well as doing this I would walk for miles around the grounds with the dogs, light a candle in the little chapel and wonder where Godmother was now. The mechanics of death nagged endlessly at me. I have never had any doubt that we do go on to another existence – I have always felt that there must be a continuation of consciousness between people who love each other in this world and the next – but at that time I kept mulling over in my mind the actual separation of the soul from the body.

I missed Godmother more and more, and all I could look forward to were Franco's visits. By now we both knew how the other felt – we had been for walks and talked together; he had told me how hard he was fighting his emotions; I admitted that I wasn't doing any such thing. He was well aware of how much the sinister atmosphere had affected us all. 'I am doing all I can to calm down Mitia, but I am now at a disadvantage because I'm so in love with you.'

I must have missed the subtleties of his feelings because he went on to explain his split loyalties, talking at length of his love and devotion for his wife and children. 'They need me so much. And it's now', he told me, 'that my work puts me in constant danger. What's more, it will get greater as the Allies advance.'

He told me that knowing and loving Godmother, an English woman, had made him realize the futility of war. He told me how his initial attraction and admiration for my father had slowly changed to distaste as he watched him scheme for his own ends, and gradually terrorize the whole house. 'You see, Caterinella,' he said, 'I'm torn on all sides and what makes my position even more difficult now is that I know you too need me.'

Now that we had discussed everything together I couldn't bear to think that I was causing him such heart-searching. In the little chapel, I would kneel and pray not to love him so much. This didn't work very well, especially as he spent so much time with us.

If Franco and I hadn't made love my story might have been slightly different. Who knows? But we did – at Valsalice, and on a day when my father had gone to Rapallo. It was siesta-time, so the house was quiet. Even the servants had gone to ground and wouldn't surface until tea-time. I was in my bedroom and, hearing footsteps, looked up to see who it was. Franco was coming slowly towards me. My heart missed a beat and I ran to his arms: 'How lovely to see you.' But he said nothing, just held me and was strangely still.

The top floor of Valsalice was made up of long corridors; at the end of one was my bedroom but, without a word, Franco pushed me away from him and guided me towards one of the guest-rooms to the right. The shutters were pulled-to over opened windows; this kept out the full heat of an Italian summer's afternoon, and the pale green half-light was beautifully cool.

Franco was in no hurry whatsoever and we lay fully-dressed on the bed together. I felt so happy as he slowly, lovingly undressed me. I was an eager, enthusiastic learner and followed my leader until we lay in peaceful exhaustion after the full rush of passion.

After a while he kissed me gently and went to get his cigarettes from the table. As he turned and smiled down on me, his expression changed to one of horror. 'Good God! You were a virgin!'

'Of course.'

'But your father said...'

'What did he say?' I was bewildered.

Franco sat on the edge of the bed, his head in his hands. 'That you already had a lot of sexual experience...'

I could hardly hear him. 'But why? How?' and I looked down at the blood on the sheets. All the joy of giving left me.

Apparently, and I shall never understand why, my father had told Franco that not only was I no longer a virgin, but that among my various sexual exploits were those with the eighty-year-old gardener. If it hadn't been so unkind, this accusation would have been funny. Gillone could hardly totter, he looked like an ancient turtle in search of a shell and his only hobby was to teach the Latin names of his beloved plants to anyone willing to learn.

I didn't want to hear any more details of my father's lies. Franco cradled me in his arms repeating, 'My poor darling. How could a father say such things about his daughter.' I clung to him desperately and felt very, very sick.

From time to time my father went off on his own to Rapallo. He called it 'tying up loose ends'. I suspected they might be linked with Augusta. He mentioned her name more often now and it was obvious that he had begun to rely on her a great deal. It wasn't until the late summer of 1944, though, that she actually moved in to Valsalice. When she did, Papa installed her in the Red Room, a huge square of a place draped with scarlet, right at the top of the house. It had a magnificent view over the park and Turin.

From the start Augusta exuded charm to Nonna, Tante Nadine and Lily and, to be fair, she made every effort to be nice to me too, but I can't pretend that I was receptive. What an incongruous situation: here was I, full of resentment and hostility towards her because I felt she had taken over Godmother's place in Godmother's home, whilst at the same time I was sleeping with my father's so-called best friend.

How my father found out about Franco and me I don't remember, but I will never forget the battle royal that followed. I reacted like a trapped wild animal, doubly fierce in its terror at a stronger opponent, and he thrashed and bellowed like a wounded bull. Blows fell hard from all sides. I hurled anything I could lay my hands on, but his aim was better than mine. At the end of it all there was a terrible amount of debris, but though decidedly battered, I was not broken. This may be because, even though I knew what I had done with Franco was wrong, I felt in a way that I had an excuse for behaving as I did.

And it was, I believe, at this stage of my life that I learnt that anything anybody does can never be painted either black or white – differing circumstances combined with individual feelings always turn actions into various shades of grey. That is why I am always ready to understand other people's mistakes, and can only feel sorry for those who feel qualified to sit in judgement.

From all points of view this was a very tricky situation. Papa understandably banned Franco from the house, but by doing this he placed himself in imminent danger. Franco knew of all my father's activities and both men were well aware that a telephone call from Franco to the right number could put Papa in front of a firing-squad before you could say 'trial'. But what they both also knew was that if my father could last the course until the Allies, who were by now advancing steadily into Italy, reached Turin, the odds were that he could turn the tables and have Franco executed.

One of the results of this state of affairs was that Papa was never seen unarmed again, and Augusta, the three old Russian ladies and I were obliged to sit through each meal with a strategically-placed and loaded revolver on the table. This Papa would brandish threateningly at the slightest unexpected sound.

I was quite convinced that Franco would not inform on my father but I was still desperately worried. I knew Nonna, Tante Nadine and Lily were concerned about me, but my instincts told me not to run to them for comfort in case it might bring Papa's wrath down on them. I could think of no way out of this vicious circle but I hid my panic behind tight lips and dry eyes. I don't know whether it would have made any difference if I'd tried to talk to my father and shown him how scared I was, but I didn't and the stubborn hostile attitude I put on to camouflage my fears only helped to build up the high, impenetrable wall between us.

I had one foolproof method of incensing my father: it was to raise an eyebrow in a quizzical, ridiculing expression. At lunch one day he announced, 'I've invited four German officers for dinner tonight and...' He would have gone on but I felt my lip curl in a silent, uncontrollable sneer. His reaction was equally quick and my cheek stung as the back of his hand slashed across my face.

'Don't you *dare* defy me,' he roared as he got up, grabbed my arm and hurled me out of the dining-room. I kept going, with him in full pursuit, until we reached my bedroom at the top of the house. Once there I whipped round to face him, but the terror I now felt inside must have appeared as rebellion on my face because he again lashed out at me – once – twice – then he turned and strode out, slamming and locking the door behind him. 'And that is where you will stay from now on,' is all I heard him say.

The days, then the weeks, crept by. My father would bring me a tray of food three times a day. He'd put it down in silence and walk out of the room without even a glance. When he did look at me I would lower my eyes and hope to God that he wouldn't take exception to my blank expression.

Once he arrived when I was leafing through my movie albums. He set down the tray and came over to me. After looking over my shoulders for a few moments he reached over and, gathering up the books, said: 'I must have a bonfire of a whole load of rubbish, these useless things will help to start it.'

'Oh, no! *Please*, Papa, I love them. Don't take them.' I ran after him with arms outstretched. 'Please,' I implored again.

'Don't be so ridiculous.' He shut the door in my face.

I'd cried so much and so often since I had been imprisoned, but never more than I did over the loss of those albums. I'd built them up with such loving care over the years and to have them confiscated and burnt at this particular moment assumed the proportions of a major tragedy. Although I was often scared and had even disliked my father, now for the first time I think I really hated him, and even after all these years, I feel regret and resentment at such mental cruelty.

Looking back now I wonder how on earth I did not go out of my mind during those three long months locked in my room. There were my books, but I'd read and re-read them, and anyway I couldn't concentrate for more than a few minutes at a time. My mind was in a turmoil, and, on top of everything else, I was positive I was dying because I could not see Franco. I would play a game of 'If'. In it I would work out all the different permutations of what could happen next. They all ended in disaster. I sometimes felt as though a boa constrictor was squeezing the life out of me.

My bedroom looked out over the front drive and I could see cars coming and going; Papa had taken the precaution of having them all turn into the side entrance to the villa, so I couldn't see who his guests were, something which made me feel even more isolated.

High on the hill opposite to Valsalice stood the Tre Gennaio (the 3rd of January). This austere-looking building was owned by the GIL (Gioventu Italiana del Littorio) and used as a holiday resort for youngsters whose parents couldn't afford to send them to the sea. I used to gaze out at it miserably, watching for some sign of life. Suddenly, one afternoon, I thought I saw movement on the road that led up the hill. Could it be a person? Yes, it was. I screwed up my eyes to focus. It was Franco. I could just make out his tall, lean figure. He was waving a white cloth wildly in the air above his head. I stifled a shout of joy. I could also make out that he was carrying a pair of binoculars. So – I reasoned – if he could see me clearly, perhaps I could get a message to him. My brain raced with hopes and plans. Why hadn't I learnt semaphore? I wondered if he had, but that wasn't a great help! He was obviously trying hard to tell me something. I understood nothing except that he was there, alive. All I could do was wave my arms about in utter frustration.

After that, Franco would come back every single day – not always at the same time, nor for very long, but it was enough to make me want to go on living. There came a point at last when I knew that I had to do something. The clockwork routine of my father's footsteps down the corridor, the key in the door, the tray he brought in and put down in silence three times a day had lasted three long months – and I couldn't take it anymore. When Franco appeared on the road the next day, I tried to 'tell' him with gestures that I was going to escape. I knew where I could go because Franco had a small flat on the far side of Turin, but how I was actually going to get out of this 'cell' was another matter.

Just below my windows there were two small balconies, and then a sheer drop of forty to fifty feet. The balconies were outside what had been Godmother's bedrooom and nobody slept there now, so this would be a bonus. If I could get down onto them, there was a narrow ledge which I could crawl along and reach the long terrace which led to the chapel. Once there, I would be in the park. Another thing to my advantage was a gigantic tree which spread across my side of the house and it was so thickly-leaved that it would give me considerable protection from being seen by the night watchman.

As actually getting away began to seem possible, I made my plans. I would wear my green suede wind-cheater over a pullover and a skirt – my father disapproved of trousers, and jeans were still to come into my life. Then I packed, Dick Whittington-style, a change of underwear, soap, toothbrush and paste, brush and comb, my rosary and prayer book and I can clearly remember adding my eau de cologne as a final 'necessity'.

My two sheets would help me reach the balconies, but tying them together wasn't easy. Every time I tugged hard they came undone. I had to tie, tug, and re-tie over and over again. At last I felt they would be safe. I had concentrated so hard that, for once, the time had flown by and my heart missed a beat as I heard Papa's footsteps approaching. When he left, I listened until I felt sure he had gone downstairs. He often walked away firmly, then tiptoed back and flung the door open again to see what I was doing.

The evening I planned to leave, it started to drizzle at about six o'clock. At eight, two cars roared up the drive and drew up outside the main entrance. Six German officers got out and ran up the stairs. The doors slammed and the chauffeurs parked the cars underneath 'my' tree.

My mouth felt terribly dry. The walls of my room were crowding in on me and I felt very, very frightened. Should I postpone my plans? No, I reasoned, even if the guests stayed late they were bound to have gone by the time I planned to leave. What's more, Papa always plied his friends generously with drink, which meant that he too would have more than usual and sleep more soundly. The servants were likely to be overtired and hear nothing either. Yes, this was still the night to get away.

All the same, when my father brought my tray in that evening, he looked so colourful in his ruby-red satin rubashka – the traditional high-necked, long-sleeved Russian tunic which suited him so well – that for a moment I had a deep pang of regret that our relationship should have disintegrated to this point. It would have taken so little for me to fling my arms round his neck, but he noticed nothing and was obviously anxious to get back to his guests.

The hours crawled by. I kept looking at the time. I got into bed, then got out again; looked out of the window, then went back to bed again. I couldn't settle but I must have fallen asleep because I woke up with a start. There were raucous goodbyes being shouted outside, then the cars drove away. It was two o'clock. Only minutes later I heard Augusta and Papa come upstairs; her steps went along the corridor, but his stopped – no doubt he was listening for sounds from my room. Hearing nothing, he followed her.

It was just after four in the morning when I made my move. The drizzle had left the balcony wet – if I slipped, would I be killed or just break a leg, I wondered? An owl hooted, a dog barked, then something rustled in the leaves below. These sounds still haunt me when I re-live that night.

There was just a glimmer of dawn light in the sky. I attached the sheets to the wrought-iron railing at my window. My few belongings were round my waist so my hands were free, and as I swung one leg over the railing I made the sign of the Cross. The sheets held firm and I dropped onto the balcony below. So far so good. The next few yards were the worst. The ledge around the wall of the house was much narrower than it had looked from above, and my shoes felt slippery. I edged along inch by inch; I didn't dare look down. The few yards between me and the corner looked like miles. At last I stretched out and clutched the stone parapet of the terrace.

My arms felt weak and woolly by now, my knees trembled and I wanted to cry, but there was no time for that. Once on the terrace I scuttled along, crouching low, towards the chapel.

Rather than open the gate I climbed back over the parapet and let myself drop into the bushes. Now I was past the point of no return. The thickly shrubbed paths gave me protection, but the shushing of leaves and crackling of twigs as I brushed through were deafening. The park had never seemed so vast when I had run round it with the dogs. Would I ever reach the wall? The *wall*! Oh God! I hadn't thought about how I was going to get over that. It was at least six feet high and two feet broad. Built with rough stones it would at least offer a foothold, but ... I had to make for the lowest point, and that was dangerously near the lodgekeeper's cottage and Cesira and Secondo, who lived there, might hear me.

I approached the lodge very steadily. There was no sign of life. Taking a deep breath I darted across the gravel and into the undergrowth. I stood still, alert for any sound – everything was quiet, so I crept on. Crouched at the foot of the wall, it looked impossible to climb over. Then I remembered there was a small gate somewhere. I found it half-hidden, overgrown with weeds and thick with rust. I tore my way through the prickly, stinging growth and felt for the crossbar. I found a foot-hold, pulled myself up and over and fell heavily into the stony road below.

I was free! My hands and legs were badly grazed and cut but this was no time to inspect my wounds. Running footsteps were approaching – hundreds of them. They came thundering past me, lots of men in different uniforms, all of them carrying guns and bayonets at the ready. Not one noticed me huddled against the wall.

Then came an explosion, and another louder one. They came from the direction of the lodge. A moment's silence was followed by screams and shouts and the rattling of machine-gun fire. What on earth was happening? On the very day I had picked to escape from home, the partisans came flooding from the hills into the city – civil war had broken out.

How I found my way to Franco's hideaway I'll never know. Maybe I would have turned back immediately if I thought my father had set up a hunt for him, but I didn't, and the three days that we stayed together in that tiny flat were the most harrowing of my life: that musty sweetness of shut-in heat; the tricks time played, flying by one moment and stopping dead the next; the box of a kitchen where I tried to prepare a little food that neither of us really wanted; and, above all, Franco's drawn and hollow-eyed expression. Everything about those days still haunts me.

He was desperately worried about his wife and children. They were still in their flat on the other side of Turin and he was aware that with this new turn of political events they could easily be taken in reprisal for his disappearance. Never once did Franco reproach me for adding so dangerously to his responsibilities. He made me feel the drastic step I had taken was the only logical one. His distress grew simply because now, as a wanted man, he could do nothing to protect me.

He had to leave me briefly the first day but after that he bolted the door saying, 'We'll have to stay quietly here.' He made one telephone call, but no one rang back. He used to hold me very tight and crush me so hard to him that his heartbeats thumped against my body – they spoke louder than any words.

Outside we could hear sporadic outbursts of machine-gun fire, and explosions. 'Hand-grenades,' he said, 'this is the greatest tragedy, blood brothers must be fighting and killing each other in the streets.'

Through the closed shutters we could see little; the street looked empty and the occasional silence was unnatural. It felt as though even the houses were holding their breath for fear of being destroyed.

At night we lay locked in each other's arms – only once did I feel his tears on my cheek and held him tight as sobs wracked his body. I kept repeating, 'Please God let us wake up dead.'

On the third morning, 29 April 1944, Franco was more ashen-faced than ever. I felt his nerves could not take much more of the strain.

'I'll have to leave you for a few hours today.' I had feared this was coming. 'I must find out what's going on. Don't answer the door or telephone – if I call, I'll ring twice and then dial again.'

He was all set to go when there was a shouted command, followed by a heavy clumping of boots on the stairs. We held our breath. They went on past our floor and on to the next landing. 'Open the door!' The voice was loud and arrogant. Someone put their finger on the bell and kept it there. 'Come on – open up.'

They were banging at the door now and after the thuds came the ear-splitting crash as the wood gave way. There was shouting, a woman shrieked then two gunshots rang out in quick succession. A split second later men thundered down the stairs and were gone. I clung to Franco and through the eerie silence from the floor above came the most pitiful, heart-rending sobs. It must have been several minutes before I opened my eyes and when I did there was a thick ribbon of dark liquid trickling slowly down the shutters. I knew it could only be blood.

Sometime during the next morning more boots thumped up the stairs; but this time it was our door that crashed open. Soldiers, they must have been partisans, invaded the place. Grim-faced, with fixed bayonets on rifles, they stood before Franco: 'Major Damone, you're coming with us.'

I will never forget that voice nor Franco's final, desperate look at me as he was pushed roughly out of the door. They were gone, but I was left behind.

The next forty-eight hours (for that was all they turned out to be) I remember only as one panic-stricken episode after another. The edges are blurred but the centres are defined with pinpoint clarity. At one stage I was running down a street with no idea of where I was going. A sudden burst of gunfire pulled me up short and I ducked for safety under a thick arch. As I peeped out I saw a girl at the window, her face contorted with rage and fear. She was yelling insults at three soldiers in the road below. They jeered back at her and made obscene gestures. Then one of them, a very large man, disappeared and came back a few seconds later clutching this sobbing, kicking virago under his arm. I cringed further into the doorway and watched in horror as each of the men brutally raped her. They then flung what now looked like a whimpering raggedy doll to one side and set off laughing amongst themselves. Almost as an after-thought, one of them turned back and, with his bayonet, slowly and deliberately slit her right up the middle before walking away again.

The next thing I remember was being thirsty. Terribly thirsty. I had no money and I found I was in a residential area so there were no cafés; I kept on walking until at last I recognized the hospital and went inside. There seemed to be a lot of confusion – nurses and doctors were rushing here and there, a soldier leant against a wall nursing a bandaged arm and I didn't like to ask anyone for anything. Someone pushed me into a waiting-room as they went by and the door shut behind me.

I sat down exhausted, and it was a minute or so before I realized that I was not alone. In the far corner of the room there was a large man slouched over two wooden chairs. He looked absolutely filthy and in need of a shave. His head was slumped forward, his flabby chins overlapping his chest, but I could feel his small bleary eyes bor-ing in to me. I smiled slightly, instinctively trying to humour him, but suddenly this grotesque mountain heaved himself up and charged. I jumped to one side. He missed me by a hair's breadth. He lunged again; again I dodged. Frantic with fear, I dived for the door screaming – no sound came out – but, just as this raving gorilla grabbed me, three male nurses burst into the room.

'Who the hell let this girl in here? The door was supposed to be locked.' There was a short frenzied fight and, when they led the man away, I realized that they had put him into a strait-jacket. I stood there stunned. People shoved past me. I heard a voice say, 'We've run out of anaesthetics.'

Then a hand grabbed me: 'Come on – you can help.' I was pro-pelled along a corridor and into a brightly-lit room.

I looked around and saw a couple of green-clad figures standing over a trolley. I felt myself manœuvred towards them and one of them picked up a corner of the sheet. He exposed a pulpy, bloody mass of skin and bone.

'This leg will have to come off,' he snapped, and the other person turned to me: 'You'll have to help hold him down.' But as I put my hand out I heard the buzzing of an electric saw and I must have passed out.

Somehow I left the hospital because the next thing I can remember clearly is the police headquarters. I'd passed the *carabinieri* on the gate – they didn't notice as there was a great commotion all round. I kept going – nothing mattered any more to me, I just had to have news of Franco. I stopped one officer and asked. He knew nothing but passed me on to another. This time the man looked at me and hesitated. 'Yes, Signorina,' he said softly, 'we've just heard. Major Damone has been executed!' I turned away and staggered across the road to a church. There I sank to my knees and sobbed my heart out.

Who knows how much later it was when I felt a hand on my shoulder and looked up. An Italian officer said very kindly. 'I've been looking for you. Why don't you let me take you home?'

Completely shattered, I leant back in the car, but as we approached Valsalice all my terror surfaced again and by the time we arrived I was completely hysterical. Secondo opened the gates and as we drove in I implored the driver not to take me up to the villa. A telephone call brought Augusta running – my Father wasn't at home – but I lashed out at her as violently as I would have done at him. She was faced with a wild cat, totally out of control. I was convinced Papa had arranged Franco's execution, so to my mind she was just his partner in crime.

By now everybody was screaming in an attempt to calm me down (after all it had been quite a day) and nobody noticed the van which drew up until a group of armed ruffians had surrounded us. While they kept everyone else covered one of them grabbed me and held me against the gate at gunpoint. 'We're going to shoot you.' he growled. 'We can do without aristocrats.'

Now it was Augusta's turn to become hysterical. She entreated their leader to go with her while she made a telephone call. To my amazement he agreed and they disappeared into the Lodge. In no time they were back. 'Let her go,' he snarled, and with a wave of his rifle he called off his men. They were gone as quickly as they'd come. Augusta, to this day, can't remember who she called, but the fact remains that she saved my life.

At this point my father's car sped into the drive – he was out of it practically before it had stopped. We glowered at each other for a split second.

'It would be better for my daughter not to come back to the Villa.'

'I'm not coming home!'

We had spoken at the same time and for once we'd agreed. He went on, 'I've arranged for her to be taken care of at the Tre Gennaio!' and turned to the police. 'Perhaps you would drive her up there in your car.' This made me more convinced than ever that he was connected with Franco's execution. He must have foreseen that I would eventually be found and brought back, so he had already planned to send me to that bleak building on the hill.

Once there they must have kept me sedated, because I have hazy memories of white walls, white curtains, white bedsteads, white uniformed nurse and little else. Then suddenly one morning I was fully conscious again. It was horrible. Everything flooded back to my mind. Godmother was dead. Franco was dead. I had no home any more and yet again I had that gnawing thought, 'Where, oh where is my mother?'

The white–clad nurse smiled at me. Her eyes were the sort that seemed to float in tears, but she looked kind and I warmed to her. 'You have to get dressed now because the car will be here soon.'

'Where am I going?'

'I'm coming with you. We are going to San Maurizio Canavese.'

Locked
Away

We pulled up outside a large, forbidding pair of solid wooden gates. The old-fashioned iron pull-bell rang out loudly, the gates were opened and we drove in. The garden looked as though it had seen more caring days and at first glance the Villa Bertalazona was a solid, no-nonsense house.

A dapper little man with obviously-dyed black hair, slicked flat to his head, wearing a white overall, was at the top of the steps leading to the front door. As we got out of the car he came forward 'washing his hands' to greet us. I noticed at once that although his lips smiled, his dark eyes remained very hard. 'I'm Professor Tam.' He sounded ingratiating.

When the nurse and driver had left, Professor Tam smarmed his way upstairs with me to the first floor and led me to the far corner of what looked like the drawing-room. He opened what I thought was an unnecessarily solid door and beckoned me to go in. 'This will be your bedroom,' he informed me.

It was quite a large room and the window overlooked the garden, but the overall effect was gloomy because of the heavy oak furniture and dark red curtains. Then I had to ask: 'Please explain Professor, who are you and what sort of place is this?'

'The Villa Bertalazona is a Casa di Salute.' He hesitated. He must have seen my expression because he said 'You must look upon it as a rest-home where you will get well again.'

I leapt up in indignation: 'But there's absolutely nothing wrong with me at all,' I said, playing straight into his hands.

'No, my dear of course there isn't!' How I loathed that syrupy, soothing manner. 'But a few months here with us will make all the difference.'

Good God! A few *months*? In a Casa di Salute! It was no good him going on about a rest-home – this was a home for the mentally unstable, and from the way he'd been treating me there was no doubt that he considered that I was fully qualified to be there.

I woke up the first morning and for an instant felt that everything must have been a nightmare, that nothing had really happened. But then, fully conscious, I realized I'd have had to go back a heck of a long way to a time I was really happy. As it was, I had to face the fact that now I was virtually on my own and in a place from where there was no chance of escape. Where would I have escaped to anyway?

What the house rules were and which ones applied to me I had yet to find out, but after breakfast I ventured into the garden without anyone stopping me. A dog joined me and seemed to want to show me around. Just as I had suspected, there was a high wall round the grounds, but it didn't worry me. Quite honestly, I wasn't planning to scale anything for the time being. Although I met nobody, I had a nagging and most unpleasant feeling that I was being watched; but, though I kept turning round quickly, I never caught a spy. I followed the paths until, after ten minutes or so, I found myself facing the house again. This time I was in front of a different wing and the windows had bars across them; I stopped and watched. I couldn't see much – the odd nurse complete with head-dress walking to and fro in the rooms; white-jacketed young men too, they must have been male nurses. That first day I saw nobody else but I occasionally heard raised voices and there was one sound which was to become very familiar – a sort of a low, moaning whimper which gradually grew into the baying howl, like a dog to the moon. I can hear it to this day and it often curdled my blood through those long, hopeless months.

Slowly, I began to realize that I was trapped once again; but the full horror of the situation only dawned on me later. What I didn't know at the time was that my father had pressed a generous sum of money on Professor Tam in return for a certificate stating that I was totally unbalanced. With this in his hand Papa was well protected from all sides. Politically no one would have believed anything I might say. Domestically he was free to flaunt Augusta with no recriminations from me. What is more, it was the perfect answer should my mother eventually query his decision to have me shut up. He could, in fact, also add that as my life had been threatened once by the Communists I was safer behind locked doors.

I thought of my mother more and more. I felt she was my only hope of salvation, but I had only a vague idea of where she was and not the slightest notion of how to contact her. All I could do at this stage was bide my time. I was so utterly exhausted that the first days just vanished in a waking sleep. It was only as I gradually began to come to life again that I started to realize what had happened to me and look back on the trail of havoc which lay behind me. The thought of Franco's widow and family haunted me night and day, and even now I wonder if they remember me with bitterness. I can only hope that something has happened in their lives to compensate for that tragedy. At that time I wanted to write but had no way of posting a letter.

My every movement was watched. Professor Tam appeared to have one principal assistant, a tall white-haired man who was so aloof that he seemed totally uncommitted to his patients. There were also a number of satellites who all wore white overalls and indulgent smiles, which made me want to shake them every time I saw them.

I was to spend nine slow months at the Villa Bertalazona. It is odd that, even though I often sank to the depths of despair, I never once thought of committing suicide. Although there was absolutely no logical way out of this situation I just prayed for a miracle and felt sure that it would eventually happen.

The Villa Bertalazona had spacious rooms and many of them, but these never seemed to light up even when the sun shone through them. There was an eerie quality about the place. At night I often heard strange cries and moans, but however far I leant out of my window I couldn't make out where they came from and if I looked up at the windows the following morning from the garden they seemed to mock me and keep their secrets.

From the number of nurses and other staff I saw around it was obvious that there were many patients at the Bertalazona but I met only a few; they were the ones who, like myself, were allowed the run of the garden and certain rooms of the house and, although observed, we weren't aggressively supervised.

As far as I was concerned – unless there were secret potions added to my food or drink that I knew nothing about – I was not given any treatment; but after I had been at the villa for a few weeks I was told that they were going to submit me to ECT or 'Electro-shock', as they called it. It meant nothing to me but when I mentioned it to one manically-depressive gentleman, his reaction made me think.

'Oh well, you'll never be the same again!' he foretold. 'It does terrible things to your memory. I won't be surprised if you don't recognize me the next day.'

'But what do they do?'

'They strap you down firmly so you can't move even an inch. Then they put a tight rubber-band round your head and attach things called electrodes to them and run currents all the way through your brain until it gets scrambled – just like eggs – and of course it never goes back to what it was.'

I decided that Electro-shock was something I could well do without. But how? Nobody was likely to listen to anything I said, asked, pleaded. The situation was worse than I could ever have feared. I had nobody else I could talk to. Everyone on the staff, although pleasant, just smiled and said, 'It's nothing – nothing at all.'

When I went to bed at night I tried to stay awake so nobody could come and take me into the treatment-room while I was asleep. There was no key in my bedroom door; I knew by now that if anyone had to stay in their rooms a key would be found and turned from the outside. In the dark I kept seeing that dyed head of Professor Tam looming above me, his sneering face zooming in on me until his evil little eyes were inches away from mine. I wanted to cry out – then didn't for fear that if I did I'd be put in that other wing with the barred windows.

A few days went by but just as I was telling myself that maybe the whole thing had been forgotten, I woke up to find one of the male nurses standing by my bedside with a hypodermic needle in his hand. Nobody could have jumped out of bed faster than I did. He didn't even try to come after me. I think I might have reacted like a trapped rat if he had done. He simply turned, left the room and came back with a larger colleague a few seconds later. By this time I had told myself that they had the whip hand, or at least the syringe, so I'd better stay as calm and as sensible as I possibly could. (Was I perhaps learning from experience to keep my cool?) Anway it worked, because I persuaded them that I'd go quietly wherever they wanted to take me if they promised not to give me an injection.

We walked to the treatment-room where Professor Tam was 'washing' his hands and talking to a nurse. He turned as we came in. 'Ah Good morning my dear!' His *bonhomie* was slimy. 'Now I do hope you realize that what we're going to do to you will be for your own good.'

I bit my lip and could not say a word.

'You just have to lie down on this table and it'll all be over in a few minutes.'

There was a white cover on the surgical bed and I saw various leather straps attached to either side of it. By now I had been slipped into a white shift and was lifted on to this contraption. The nurse put some sticky solution on to my temples, then into my hair. It felt horrible, but what could I do? I kept telling myself that my father couldn't possibly have ordered them to kill me but, trapped like this, I began to wonder what death would be like. The image of Franco flashed through my mind. Did it hurt to be shot? But I was being electrocuted. Although I'd been scared before, this seemed to be happening in slow motion, which made it a thousand times worse. All the same, I could not let anyone see my fear. But what did it really matter? It was just that I hated the thought of scrambled brains.

I felt the strap tighten round my wrists and ankles. I was sure they could hear my heart-beats. Now my head had a band round it. Wires reached out to me from an octopus-like machine. How I wished I'd let the nurse give me a black-out injection. I also wished they'd get on with things. I knew I was going to scream – I couldn't hold back any more.

Then, suddenly, there were some muffled whispers. I felt the wires were being tugged and re-adjusted. Flat on my back I couldn't see anything, but felt that things weren't going according to plan. I held my breath ... the machine had broken down. A little later I was escorted back to my room and, although I lived in dread of it, no one ever mentioned ECT again.

As the months dragged by I noticed two other people who didn't appear to like the Professor any more than I did. They were the owners of the Villa Bertalazona, Commendatore and Signora Cordiglia. A comfortable-looking couple in their sixties, they took no part in the running of the place and lived in a separate wing, but when the days grew shorter in the autumn they came and joined a few of us in the drawing-room after supper. The old boy would puff at his pipe and I could see his bright eyes darting around taking everything in. Then I began to notice that when Tam appeared for his goodnight round neither of them would say a word to him, and once or twice I caught a look between husband and wife which made me think.

'Would you like to make up a foursome at Scopa?' the Signora asked me one evening. Though not mad about cards, I agreed and discovered they were both warm, friendly people with a reassuring sense of humour. Then they discovered I loved jigsaw puzzles and, the next day, I found a big table set up in the drawing-room with an enormous puzzle they'd dug out of the attic for me. I think they sensed how grateful I was because there were times when I was quite convinced I was going slowly but surely mad.

It was late one night that a key turned in my door and Mrs Cordiglia came into my room. She sat on my bed and took my hand.

'You've probably noticed that both my husband and I have become very fond of you, and we would like to help you.'

'In what way?' Although I liked them I couldn't help but be wary.

'Well, we don't think you should be in this place and we're prepared to see if we can get you out.'

'Escape?'

'No, not exactly. You've often mentioned your mother and I

gather she doesn't know you are here. If we could get in touch with her I'm sure she would come and see you.'

'But how?'

'I don't quite know, but my husband and I are going to find out who we should contact if you can give us her name and address.'

'Name, yes, but I only know that she is in a hotel in Switzerland. Please, please help me to find her!'

'Now don't get too excited and above all don't breathe a word to anyone.' I promised and, as she crept out of my room, I allowed myself to have a tiny glimmer of hope.

With more than a touch of cloak-and-dagger I slipped into the Cordiglias' wing of the house, then out through their private door into their car. Within seconds the three of us were speeding along the road to Turin.

'We are taking you to the Allied Military Government Headquarters.' said Mr Cordiglia. His voice sounded strained. 'Your English is good, no?'

'My English is good, yes.'

'We are going to see a senior American officer, who will be able to help us find your mother.' There was a bulldog quality about Mr Cordiglia which I found reassuring. He seemed determined that everyone was going to be on my side now. Mrs Cordiglia held my hand. I held my breath. This was my one chance to do something about my life, but I was worried stiff that these two kind old people would get into serious trouble because of me.

The AMG headquarters were set up in one of Turin's smartest hotels. Surrounded by men in uniform, we must have looked an odd and bewildered trio – a lanky blonde between two elderly people dressed in their shabby Sunday best.

'You want to see Captain Taylor?' Without waiting for an answer someone swept us along a corridor towards an open door.

'Come right on in,' came a friendly drawl. And there we were in front of a large desk and an even larger American officer.

'I'm Captain Taylor – Tom Taylor from Tennessee,' he grinned broadly. 'What can I do for you all?'

After bursting into a flood of tears I gave him Mama's name, a list of her possible whereabouts and swore him to secrecy. Then Mr Cordiglia drove like a dervish back to Bertalazona. I tried so hard not to get despondent, and the Cordiglias were a great comfort, but I was miserable. The end of 1944 was approaching and I was dreading the idea of Christmas in prison. It was no easy task I'd set Captain Taylor and I didn't dare hope that I would hear from him before the New Year. I wrote to my father asking him to send me a pair of shoes from my cupboard, and on an impulse of goodwill sent him my best wishes for Christmas.

The telegram I received in return stunned me:

I RETURN YOUR BEST WISHES FOR CHRISTMAS AND INFORM YOU OF MY MARRIAGE TO AUGUSTA. I SHALL SEND YOU THE SHOES YOU HAVE ASKED FOR. DEMETRIO IMPERIALI.

My father had completely deserted me.

Lost and Found

The waiting was agony. Would Captain Taylor locate my mother? And if he did, would she care? Papa had told me so often that she did not. Why had she never written? But then how many letters of hers had been torn up without me knowing? And again, if she could not be found, would I be left at the Bertalazona for ever? Doubts, hopes and fears chased each other around wildly in my muddled mind.

One morning I was summoned to Professor Tam's office, and suddenly my mother was there. She was smaller and prettier than I remembered – six years between the ages of twelve and eighteen is a very long time. For a fraction of a second I stood rooted in the doorway, then her arms reached out and I fell into them. When we had recovered a degree of composure, she introduced me to a man called Dottore Pecorella. Stocky and sharp-featured, with glasses, he was her solicitor and had travelled from Rome to meet her. I felt reassured to have him there because I knew my father would erupt when he heard that Mama had arrived.

From the start he played 'dog in the manger'. The last thing he wanted was to have me back home, especially now that he was newly-wed; but he was damned if my mother was going to have me either. He played his trump card at once: the letter for which he had paid Professor Tam so highly and which stated that I was unbalanced and could therefore not be removed from the Bertalazona. But he reckoned without, or maybe under-rated, my mother's

Yorkshire grit combined with the abilities of this particular legal eagle.

Although Pecorella could not get me to Rome as he would have wished, he arranged for two psychiatrists to come and examine me at the villa. I cannot remember their names, but I shall never forget their methods. I was sat on a hard stool for what seemed to be hours on end, with a sharp light focussed on my face: then they cross-examined me. I must have been put through every I.Q. and physical reaction test in the book; they explored every nook and cranny of my mind. They felt the bumps on my skull; they strapped bands round my head, bands round my arm, and they tapped my ankles, wrists and knees. I had never heard of the Devil's Advocate, but I was up against two of them. At times, as a cowed criminal must do, I wanted to cry out for leniency, but didn't. Something deep inside me said 'Stay calm'; it kept telling me I was perfectly sane, and if I kept a tight grip on myself, this all-important truth would out. This was my fight for freedom, and I had to win.

For two – or was it three? – days we were closeted in that room. Then, just when I was utterly worn out and could take no more ... they were gone. Instead, Mama and Pecorella stood there, smiling. She handed me a piece of paper. 'Read that, my darling. There is absolutely nothing wrong with you.' As an afterthought, she practically spat out, 'I knew there wasn't.'

I did not know I was crying, but I suddenly felt tears scalding my cheeks. It felt odd to be in the wide-open world again, and it took a little time to realize that I had no need to feel frightened any more.

Mama and I stayed in Turin for a few nights. At that early stage freedom was still a bit overwhelming, so I was delighted when Mama suggested that we share a double-room with twin beds (I did not realize then that she was also counting the pennies) and, according to her, those nights were memorable. She never slept a wink. Apparently I either ranted, raved, sobbed, sighed, or stomped about the room like a young elephant in search of its herd. I am sure it was a wretched experience for a loving mother to see her child so subconsciously distraught, and frightening because she did not dare wake me up; but I still think it conjures up a very funny picture, especially as I remembered nothing in the mornings.

From Turin we went to Rome – we knew we would feel safer further away from my father and closer to Pecorella whilst the various formalities were being completed. We travelled by train and, though the war was over, there were still a lot of men in uniform everywhere. Their faces were drawn and tired; bombed buildings and mountains of rubble had their own sad stories to tell. The emotions of the outside world had passed me by at the Bertalazona, and suddenly I felt guilty at feeling happy. When the train drew in to Civitavecchia a small group of people were huddled on the station waiting to meet a coffin off our train, and I shall always remember the desperate expression of the young woman who reached out her black-gloved hand to touch it.

Before we could leave for Switzerland there were a few hiccups in the formalities; one was caused by my being Hungarian, another by being a minor and Mama having allowed my father to have legal custody of me. 'I should never have done such a thing,' she kept saying, 'but I really did think it was for your good – your father, with Godmother's help, was able to give you a far better education than I could have afforded. And then there was the war.'

Those weeks of waiting did not worry me unduly. Mamma and I were getting to know each other again, and it was a joy to feel that, apart from anything else, we were beginning to like each other tremendously. My mother had a lively mind, a marked sense of fun and humour and, above all, a great love of books. 'I absorb print,' she used to say. Anything to do with British history, biographies and autobiographies appealed to her. On this rescue mission she had brought Lytton Strachey's *Queen Victoria* and Mrs Gaskell's *Life of Charlotte Brontë*, for company.

She loved clothes and was quietly chic, although she was now forced to live on a small fixed income in Switzerland. Mamma did not mention to me at that time that her husband was not rich; all I knew was that his name was Hyacinth (Giacinto), which made me laugh, and that he was mad about music.

What I found really remarkable about my mother was her attitude towards me after all she had been through. Instead of turning into a possessive mother, which would have been quite understandable, she wanted me from the very start to develop along my own lines.

'Do stop saying "thank you",' she would say. 'A child has nothing to thank her parents for. You never asked to be brought into this world. It was I who wanted you so badly. It was purely selfish.' This astonished me. She had no time for parents who regarded their children as some kind of investment for their old age and who expected them to be forever grateful for doing what she considered was merely part and parcel of the duty of a parent.

Eventually we left Rome for Lausanne. I had often made this trip before to Brillantmont but this time, as the train drew out of the station, I knew that I was on my way to a new life.

Mama's husband, Giacinto Scelsi, was waiting for us in the hall of the Hôtel de la Paix. I had thought it strange that he had not been at the station to meet us, and wondered if this meant I was unwelcome. There was little warmth in his greeting to Mama.

He was a stooped, grey-haired little man – I would guess in his late forties – who wore faintly-tinted glasses and had a high-pitched voice with a built-in whine. Mama explained that he wrote modern music. She said he had a lot of talent, but did not add 'and a rich American girlfriend too'. I was prejudiced against him from the moment I saw that my mother was not happy. She made every excuse for his late-night returns to the hotel, and blamed their separate rooms on his frequent 'artist's headaches'. However I felt there was a lot more than this wrong with their relationship.

Mama had lived at the Hôtel de la Paix since the beginning of the war, and had seen no reason to change when she got married. She said it was easier to have an hotel suite with an all-in arrangement than a home of their own. Her natural nesting instinct only eventually surfaced when she was happily married to her third husband. Subsequent to her divorcing my father, she had retreated to the Carlton Hotel in Cannes where, if not accompanied by a husband, at least she had a lady's maid.

Despite our cool reception, there was great excitement generally (in which, again, Scelsi did not seem to share) because we arrived from Italy at the same time as the proofs of Mama's book, from London. To try and mask her worries about what was happening to me in Italy and to her mother in England, Mama had sat down and written a very funny novel about this peaceful oasis, Switzerland – and in particular Lausanne – in war-torn Europe. Her literary agents, Curtis Brown, had had no difficulty in getting *Randolph's Folly* published. The only worry now was how many writs might follow the sometimes only lightly-veiled characters. Luckily, after some careful editing, none did; the book went on to enjoy a morale-boosting success.

Lausanne, considered dull by many people who lived there, was to me, after the life I had led, the most wonderful place in the world. Admittedly, the social life appeared to revolve around having tea with ex-Queen Ena of Spain, an assortment of other ex-crowned heads, and rich Greeks and their entourages, but I found so much else to do and see as well. Just walking around Lausanne, Ouchy and Vevey was a treat. I was able to hop on a little ferry and travel along the lake as far as Montreux and the Château de Chillon with all its Byronic memories one way, then go as far as Geneva the other. Or I sailed straight across Lac Leman to France – this was freedom, and this is what I treasured.

There were concerts, art exhibitions, theatres and cinemas to go too, but I soon realized that Mama's 'fixed' income was being strained to include me, let alone the extras in our life. This was a totally new experience for me. I had never known what it meant to count the pennies. Everything I had wanted, I had had. I had never heard the expression 'we can't afford it'. Nevertheless, I took to this very different state of affairs coolly. Maybe I simply did not want to be a burden on my mother in any way. I would play games with myself by going window-shopping – adding up all the things I especially liked, then thinking of all that money I had saved her.

I would have been quite happy to stay on in Switzerland indefinitely, but for Mama Lausanne was simply a stepping-stone to London. It was in London that she was determined I should live.

'But what will you do?' I asked. 'You're not going to leave me there on my own, are you?' Freedom could be carried too far.

'Don't worry, darling, it will become much easier to go to and fro across the Channel by plane.'

I was not reassured. I knew Mama had been amongst that small band of intrepid people who had flown from the very start of civil aviation, but in those days private individuals did not pop in and out of aeroplanes as they do now. The idea of losing a mother when I'd only just found one didn't appeal to me. She just laughed, however, and kept writing letters to her friends in England.

White plans were being laid in London, Mama was faced with having to dress me for the occasion. She had dreamt of doing this for years, but her generosity clashed stubbornly with those slender purse-strings. One night, when she thought I was asleep, I found her sitting up in bed, her little cash-book in her hand, with tears trickling down her cheeks – the francs and centimes just would not stretch to include a suit that she had set her heart on for me. Two evening dresses were also among her priorities: 'Darling, the "London Season" will make a come-back – I do want you to enjoy it,' was how she explained away what I felt to be an extravagance. 'And it will save all those coupon-counting problems in England.'

Incredible though it may sound, it was a great treat to have new clothes of my own. Papa and Godmother had had an unlikely quirk, although the war-time shortages might have been in part to blame: they had insisted that more often than not I should wear Godmother's altered cast-offs.

During this time, my stepfather was making an effort to be pleasant; but I always felt he'd put the flag out when we left. This worried me only because I guessed that Mama minded, although she changed the subject when I tried to discuss it.

Then, suddenly, in no time at all it seemed, the permits arrived; we packed, and were off to the airport. In those days, the flight from Switzerland took something like three hours, I think, but my nose was still squashed to the porthole as we landed. The airport was Northolt, just off the A40, and Britain looked bleak under a steady drizzle.

When all the other passengers had left, we were still there and Mama was getting tetchy. 'I wish to heavens you were not Hungarian,' she said for the umpteenth time. 'Yes, of course she is my daughter' – this was snapped at an official who came towards us.

'You have been out of Britain throughout the war, I believe?' He was thumbing his way through Mama's British passport.

'I have been living in Switzerland – a neutral country.'

81

'I see,' he pondered, 'I believe your husband is Italian?'

'Yes, but he never moved from Switzerland either.'

'But your daughter was in Italy.'

'Yes, she was with her father.'

'An Italian?'

'Yes, no, he took Hungarian citizenship.' It had begun to sound far too complicated.

My mother's voice was getting higher and higher. 'This is quite ludicrous. I was assured that when we arrived in England that this document would explain the situation.' She flourished an official-looking piece of paper which he had already returned to her. It left the man unmoved.

'I think you had better come with me.' He still held onto our passports. We were ushered into a small room, and the door was closed. The minutes ticked by. I supposed that at best they would pack us off back to Switzerland, at worst slap us in prison.

'Don't worry, Catherine.' Mama was obviously worried stiff.

At last the official came back, and there was another man with him. 'I am very sorry, madam, but although you can stay in England we do not seem to have had confirmation of this permit, so your daughter will not be allowed into the country.'

After Mama had made some agitated telephone calls, it was Howard Kerr who came to the rescue. He was then equerry to the Duke of Gloucester, and had been attached to the Royal Family for many years. He, his wife Christine and his sister Marie were all close, long-standing friends of Mama's. On Howard's assurance, H.R.H. Prince Henry very kindly vouched that the two distressed females at Northolt were no potential threat to Britain's safety.

So, bearing, as it were, the 'royal seal of approval', we finally left the airport. It was dark by now, and still drizzling as we drove into London.

This was London 1946 and clothing-coupons and rationing were still very much in evidence. The Basil Street Hotel, although eminently respectable, was decidedly drab. The rooms were shabby, the paint-work cracked, and the curtains and carpets seemed to have a layer of dust on them. There was no soap in the bathroom, the towels were small and always damp, and the only chambermaid we saw, although friendly, looked utterly exhausted. It was this tired look, which everyone seemed to have, that first struck me about London; the second was the strong 'stick to the rules' attitude that was quite different from Italy, where queues were made to jump. In London people waited patiently in shops, on buses, and took their turn. I got this tremendous feeling of fairness and honesty in England. I felt safe.

One rarely makes a clean break from the past. Even if we decide to emigrate, as a rule we take with us some useful possessions and stay in touch with friends and relatives. But when the axe fell on the first twenty years of my life, I had only two small treasures to show for them – a white rosary in a tiny sharp-edged tin box, and a 'Garden of the Soul' missal that Godmother had given me ten years before. She had written on the inside: 'To Caterinella. May her little heart always be a garden of faith, love and truth.' Even my precious green suede wind-cheater, in which I had escaped from Valsalice, had fallen to bits from constant hard wear. Mama had persuaded me to throw it out, rather than keep it as a relic.

There were no faces from the past around me, and nobody in Italy knew our address. It also seemed highly unlikely that I would ever go back to Italy. I discovered that when people in England ask you about yourself, they do not really want to know the answer. This made it much easier for me to pack my past into a trunk and put it into the attic of my mind. I'll sort it out one day, I told myself.

At Mass, the Sunday following our arrival, as if to confirm my resolution, the priest said: 'The past makes us what we are, but we must live in the present – make the most of the present in order to shape the future.' The words may look trite in black and white, but the Jesuit spoke them with fire, and I was eager to agree.

It was at this time that Howard's sister, Marie Kerr (who had married a cousin with the same surname as her own), stepped onto the scene. Marie had been widowed when she was very young, and her son Peter succeeded his cousin Philip (the British war-time Ambassador to Washington) after his father died, to become Marquess of Lothian. Still unfamiliar with the complicated way that

British titles work, it struck me as odd that whilst her elder son was Lord Lothian, and her younger son Lord John Kerr, she should be simply Mrs Andrew Kerr.

But, by any name, this would be a remarkable and lovable family. Marie is now a lively great-grandmother in her mid-eighties, and it is one of her daughters, Toni Lothian, who has, for the last twenty-five years, master-minded and been Chairman of the famous 'Woman of the Year Luncheon', held annually at the Savoy in aid of the Greater London Fund for the Blind.

Anyway, back in 1946, Marie lent us her delightful flat just off St James's Street. It was from there, and helped by all the Kerrs, that Mama introduced me to London. The 'Season', as Mama had predicted, was making a strong come-back after the war, and she was determined that, before she went back to Switzerland, I should make new friends and meet as many people as possible.

'You must lead a normal life from now on,' was her cry. So I was whisked off to women's luncheons at Claridges and other similar hotels, where mothers displayed their daughters to each other and swopped lists of eligible young men. I went to dinners before dances, where hostesses carefully picked and shuffled suitable partners. The tiny Sir Egerton and the formidable Lady Hamond-Graeme ('Ham and Eggs' of course) were stars on this scene.

I met chinless wonders; coped with 'taxi-tigers'; learnt that 'I'm having a MAHvellous time' said with lack of interest meant that the party was great; and that the British mistrust exuberance and 'Foreigners'. I discovered that the marriage-market was large, the goods varied, and that the Queen Charlotte Ball was Show Ring No. 1. On that night, a herd of 'young things' in long white dresses would sweep down the wide staircase, round the Grosvenor House ballroom, and dip into a deep Court curtsey before a mammoth multi-tiered iced cake. In my days, tiara'd Lady Hamond-Graeme would wield a large knife and distribute crumbling currant-bun-size slices. Since this annual occasion commemorated Queen Charlotte's Maternity Hospital, each girl would receive a stork-engraved medal as a memento.

Those were the days when young men who wanted to take you out came to collect you at home and met mother, then delivered you back, however much later, intact. A kiss on the lips at the end of an evening was daring. I found, as I'd expected, that my sexual experiences with Franco had been very special – a soft nest surrounded by barbed-wire – and I had no urge to renew them with others.

Night-clubs such as the 400 Club, the Milroy and Churchills were all the rage, and Mama gave me a twenty-first birthday party at the Bagatelle – Edmundo Ros land. How far away Italy seemed to us both that evening.

Of course this kind of life sounds hilariously old-fashioned now, but at the time, and especially under the circumstances, it was for me all a glorious adventure. My only worry was that Mama was spending money she could not afford.

The only thing I hated about England was the weather. Far too young and uninterested to think the constant drizzle and damp were good for my complexion, I fought a losing battle against straight hair (I then had one of those perms of the day which made me look as if I had put my finger in the light socket), and spent most of my time shivering. Mama laughed at me when I was still swathed in wool in mid-August; and I certainly never forgave the young man who growled at me in a downpour when I suggested he should open his tightly-rolled umbrella. 'Good heavens, girl. It belonged to my grandfather!' he said, expecting me to understand as he waved it ineffectually for a taxi.

It feels odd to be writing about Britain as a foreigner now that I have become so much a part of this country – but a foreigner is what I was. My mother spent her time being horrified by some of her 'foreign' daughter's reactions. But it was ignorance not rudeness that made me call Scotland the 'North of England', and Eton 'that little school for boys, near Windsor', and it was surprise that made me laugh at all those top-hatted, penguin-style youngsters gathered together to celebrate the 4th of June. The trouble was that, even then, I spoke English with no accent, so such behaviour was not always forgiven because 'She's only a foreigner'.

London was emerging from the enforced doldrums of a shattering war. Nothing was going to rush her. Sometimes I felt that I was the only one always in top gear, running whilst others walked.

How infuriating, tiring and even alarming I must have been to my new and more lethargic friends. But there were those who encouraged me – Johnny Kerr, for instance. I never knew whether he was laughing at or with me. With his wicked sense of the ridiculous, he once made a date to meet me, complete with roller-skates, at the top of the Mall. Dead-pan, he informed me 'On 1 May, by tradition, we skate up to the Palace and back!' It was the same Johnny who dared me to scale a Soho lamp-post – which I did, to the mild surprise of a passing policeman, who unhitched me from the top where I had got stuck. What silly, harmless fun we had. Johnny, these days Sotheby's world expert on rare books and a pure Dickensian character to look at, retains the sharpest sense of humour, but now his eyes twinkle from behind a profusion of greying whiskers.

Far too quickly, the time came for Mama to go back to Switzerland; although 'Hyacinth' was not exactly sending 'Come home quick' messages. She was loath to admit that there was anything wrong with her marriage, and wanted to do all she could to keep it going. Before she left, somewhere had to be found for me to live. It was not too difficult. There were a number of highly-respectable widows dotted around London at that time (no doubt there still are), willing to take in foreign girls as 'paying guests'. As their house or flat was often too big for them alone, this arrangement suited all parties – empty rooms were filled, the money came in useful, and the girls' parents felt that their offspring were not only in safe hands, but also had acquired a certain 'background' in the big city.

I was entrusted to Madame de Zulueta. She lived in Elvaston Place, just off Queensgate. Dora de Zulueta's husband, Philip, had been attaché to the Spanish embassy, and when I moved in her daughter Ann, a tall, good-looking blonde rather on the large side, was on the threshold of her marriage to Jaime Russo. Peter, her equally handsome son, was still only eighteen, and quite a few years away from his marriage to Daphne du Maurier's daughter.

For my room, which I shared, Mama paid in advance the princely sum of £7 a week. This included a generous breakfast and an evening meal, plus all meals over the weekend, if I wished. My room was large, overlooked the terrace onto Elvaston Place and had three beds in it. I shared it for the first few months only, with a girl called Elizabeth Kelly, whose father was British ambassador to Brussels at the time.

Mama went carefully into our finances. She bought me the basic clothes she could afford, and by the time she left, I had a Midland Bank account with £20 in it for emergencies, my first ever cheque book, and an allowance of £3 per week. Since it was obvious that I was going to have to earn my own living as soon as possible, Mama also found time to enrol me on a six-month course at Pitman's College in Russell Square, to learn shorthand and typing.

Once again, life had changed abruptly.

New
Beginnings

Although I missed Mama there was something exciting about being alone in London. Of course I knew I had the Kerrs to run to if I got into any serious trouble, but I was determined to get on with my life without being a nuisance to them.

It wasn't as easy as I had thought it would be, getting up every morning at 6.45 a.m. and trekking off on bus and tube to Russell Square; especially as that first winter was the notoriously bitter one of 1946. As for shorthand and typing, I felt it would never sink in. I knew these shorthand squiggles would never make sense; then, just as I was about to throw in the sponge and apply for a job behind a counter, all of a sudden they did. What a wonderful feeling it was. I was a shorthand-typist. How ridiculously proud I was of this achievement.

I wrote to Mama saying that I felt equipped to earn my living now with my Pitman's Certificate, and my three languages. The world was my oyster. I had immediate and spectacular visions of becoming a very private secretary to a dishy man of world-wide importance.

Where to begin? I scanned *The Times* for tempting offers; I made lists and wrote letters for interviews. Then, going off at a tangent in my usual way. I applied for a job as an air stewardness with BOAC. Of course, I had no doubt whatsoever that the 'Powers that Be' would welcome me with open arms. What is more, I thought the interview went off brilliantly. I chatted brightly and non-stop; I exhibited my eagerness to please; and spoke of my flying experience – one trip across the Channel! I left the interview on a cloud, in my mind's eye already fitted into their uniform and visualizing myself putting passengers and pilot at their ease on a particularly bumpy flight with coffee and charm.

To my utter astonishment, they turned me down! I was so stunned that I had to read the letter three times. I can't quite remember all the wording, but one line stood out. It said: 'We feel your character may be a little too lively for this responsible job.'

What a bitter blow to my pride and my ambitions. With no alternative in the offing I went down my less glamorous list of jobs again; but before I set off for my next interview, I decided to buy a hat.

The Misses Swerling had run a flourishing millinery business on a first floor in Bond Street for years. They had always been very helpful to Mama, and seemed to inherit me with pleasure. On this particular day, they just let me roam around, trying on anything and everything. I was so engrossed in what I was doing, that it was a while before I noticed a man leaning against a wall looking at me. He smiled and came closer. 'You look as though you are having fun.'

'I am,' I said and smiled back.

'I'm writing an article for *Woman's Own* about how a girl chooses a hat – would you mind if I used you as a model? We will pay you a modelling fee,' he added.

'Of course you will do it, dear,' A Miss Swerling came bustling by and made up my mind for me.

Then a lean, smart greyhound of a woman joined us. She looked me up and down, was obviously not impressed and said rather impatiently, 'Oh really, Beverly, we must use a professional model. This is just one of those debs. She probably sleeps till ten, and even if she does turn up for the appointment, she will be late.'

My hackles rose. 'I assure you I am extremely punctual. What is more I'm quite used to getting up very early.' I did not go into the subject of my threadbare finances which would welcome the fee.

She shrugged and walked away, while 'Beverly' soothed my ruffled feathers and made an appointment at a photographic studio for the following day.

Little did I know that this chance meeting would set me on the path to a modelling career – something I had never even thought of. 'Beverly' turned out to be none other than the writer Beverly Nichols, and the woman was Barbara Back. Barbara, a well-known and extremely competent journalist, set herself a high standard of discipline and expected the same from anyone she worked with; she resented those she spittingly called 'amateurs'. But once she realized that I was one of the world's workers, she was unstinting in her apologies for her initial rudeness and became a kind and wonderful friend.

At the time I thought that these amazing events were entirely due to luck, but over the years I have gradually realized that what is often called 'luck' is instead the ability to recognize a good opportunity and to grab it with both hands.

Having taken my first step towards a career in full-time modelling, however, other major events then intervened. It was at this point, in fact, that I met Richard Boyle at a friend's birthday party. A captain in the Irish Guards, he was six feet two inches tall, had reddish hair and the distinguished face of a young Punch. The fact that he was a viscount was completely overshadowed for me by the name 'Boyle'. In my Italian mind I saw it spelt 'Boil' and thought it quite hideous. What is more, I could only look blank when asked whether he was one of the Scottish or Irish Boyles. It meant nothing to me that Boyle is the family name of the Earls of Glasgow, Cork and Orrery, and Shannon; Richard's father was then Lord Shannon. What I saw, however, was a tall young man who wore his uniform well, and I thought he was the kindest, gentlest person I had ever met. It was his combination of ponderous calm and apparent strength that made me care for Richard.

Our potential incompatibility must have already been obvious to others; I have so often been asked why we ever got married. I think it was the very differences in our characters which appealed to me most in our relationship at the start. He was the opposite of my father in every way, and that Freudian link there is supposed to be between fathers and daughters must have acted subconsciously in me and drawn me towards Richard. Anyway, I'm quite sure that given the same circumstances we would always have got married. There is no doubt that there was genuine affection between us; this has been proved many times over the years by the fact that we are still real friends, and although we spent our seven years of married life infuriating each other, I *liked* Richard and always will.

Whereas I have always been an extrovert, Richard is a very private person, and at the age of twenty-one I was definitely grown up, whilst Richard was still a very immature twenty-three-year-old. His childhood, although completely different from mine, hadn't been happy. His father had married a British lawyer's daughter in India and they lived in Calcutta, where Lord Shannon was steward at the Calcutta Race Course. Richard was sent to school in England and, from the time he went to Eton, he made his headquarters at Ashe Park near Basingstoke, which belonged to his cousin Michael Boyle. I think both Richard and I longed to put down roots of our own and this was the common ground on which we met.

When I told Mama about Richard she shot back to England. Although delighted with his coat of arms she regretted it wasn't backed with gold. In fact Richard had only his army salary plus the smallest of allowances from his equally hard-up father. All the same, Mama encouraged us to get married. She felt I'd be in 'safe hands', and she often said she would feel I was really out of my father's reach when I changed my name.

Our engagement was duly announced in both *The Times* and the *Telegraph* and although I didn't know it at the time, it stirred my father into action again. Having read the announcement, he promptly wrote off to my future in-laws to inform them that their one and only son was embarking on the most unsuitable marriage to a morally unstable girl. To their eternal credit the Shannons took no notice whatsoever. They simply set aside Papa's heavily-embossed writing-paper and showed the letter to us only three or four years later. 'We felt he was rather eccentric,' was their only comment.

Unfortunately Bob and Marjorie Shannon couldn't afford to come from India for the wedding, but sent an affectionate telegram on the day. It was a small, simple occasion on a sunny September day at the Church of the Holy Redeemer in the heart of Chelsea. Father Philip de Zulueta, a cousin of my other 'de Zu's', performed the ceremony, Richard cut a distinguished figure in his Brigade of Guards uniform and I wore a long, white satin gown with gardenias in both my bouquet and my head-dress. From the church we went to Thurloe Place where Marie and Howard Kerr's mother (who was over eighty) had kindly lent her house for the reception.

Mama and I shed a few tears, of course, and as I turned to walk down the aisle my eyes held hers. I knew our minds had flown back to that day, not so very long ago, when she arrived to rescue me from the Villa Bertalazona. What a different place the world had become, and although she'd never wanted to hear me say it, my heart cried out a thank you to her yet again.

Richard and I set off for our honeymoon at Rozel Bay on Jersey in a De Havilland Rapide left over from the war – a tiny six-seater, incredibly uncomfortable and dangerously draughty. However, Rozel Bay, when we got there, was marvellously unspoilt. The weather was lovely and we spent a happy relaxed time. We both enjoyed the idea of being married and, as we watched the sun setting into the sea, like all other newly-weds we made plans for the future.

As we had nowhere to live in London, it was lucky that Richard was posted to Armagh and I could go with him. I couldn't quite believe that Armagh, with its cobblestoned main street, was one of Northern Ireland's most important towns. It looked more like a glorified village to me. But the two cathedrals, one Protestant and the other Catholic, were certainly very impressive.

This was not only my first taste of being an army wife, but also my very first glimpse of what army life was all about. I can't pretend that I took to it immediately. I spent the first few weeks feeling either overawed or irritated. Everyone, as far as I was concerned, took themselves far too seriously and the rigid, all-embracing etiquette was at times laughable. I'm sure they would have been horrified if they'd seen Richard covering a circular piece of cardboard with some black velvet to make a Dorothy-bag for me before we set off to a ball at Government House, Hillsborough, given by Lord Granville for a very young and attractive Princess Margaret.

After a few months in Armagh, Richard was posted to Palestine. Wives weren't welcome, and as I was having an uncomfortable pregnancy I set up home in London with Anne Macdonald when Richard set off to the Middle East.

Anne had come to England from the Argentine about the same time as I arrived from Italy. We both came from broken homes and had left behind rich fathers who had financially washed their hands of us. What with this and our Latin upbringing, we immediately found we had a lot in common and became fast friends. Anne was outstandingly pretty – she still is – but at twenty she looked like one of those exquisite dolls you unwrapped from layers of tissue paper, and then just gazed at because they were far too fragile to play with. Despite her ethereal exterior, and the quietest and most unhurried voice, Anne was a very capable, determined young woman. When we shared a small mews flat in Pavilion Road, it was she – and not the practical-looking me – who ran the place and kept us both within our very limited budgets. The flat belonged to a Spanish marquess, Julio de Amodio; it was minute and inappropriately full of heavy Empire furniture with lots of dark-red silks and satins. Most of one room was taken up by an outsize Napoleonic bed, on which some of our most successful dinner parties were held – a brass tray in the middle and two guests on each side of it.

This was a limbo kind of time. Young and married but minus a husband, I resented being pregnant, above all because it made me feel so ill. With Richard away, my idea had been to get out, find an interesting job and start earning some money. Instead I was wasting half of each day being wretchedly sick, even after six months. All the same, when I accidentally hurtled down our short, steep flight of stairs and landed up in St Mary's Hospital, Paddington, it was an emotional and painful shock to lose the baby.

I have a kaleidoscope of memories of the months that followed. At home I played confidante to a string of love-sick swains – Anne bowled over the boys like ninepins and I rather enjoyed my role of understanding married chaperone.

I was still stage-struck and, at the back of my mind, still determined to have something to do with show business in one way or another. I jumped at the chance therefore when a rich Greek invited me to meet a film producer over dinner at the Ritz. I dressed to kill – the dress was long, of course. When I arrived I was slightly surprised

93

to be told that Mr G. was waiting for me in his suite. Determined, however, not to seem unsophisticated, I smiled and swept into the lift and up to the suite. The door opened and I was most graciously received by my host; but one glance at the candlelit table laid for two, the champagne on ice and, through a half-open door, the king-size bed invitingly turned down told me at once that no producer would be joining us. My poise evaporated, I turned tail and, with my dress hitched up to my knees, fled along the corridor, down the impressive staircase into the hall, out of the main door and on to a passing bus. I didn't care where it was going.

The next morning, to my utter astonishment, a slender package was delivered from Cartier's. I opened it and in a black velvet-lined red case lay the most magnificent diamond bracelet. I naturally returned it to the Ritz with a note. It came back again. I returned it once more. It came back again, and again, and again. I wrote and told Richard all about this incident and in his reply he suggested that perhaps, after all, I deserved to keep it. (Later, when times were tough, the money from the sale of the bracelet kept me for a year.)

It was around this time that I was introduced by one of the (it seemed to me) innumerable Boyle aunts to another member of the family – Patrick Boyle. A cousin of Richard's, balding, bespectacled, nearing forty and a confirmed bachelor, he was considered to be a very suitable escort for me. He was writing and drawing for *Punch* magazine, and had just published a book on his experiences as a Chindit in the Far East. He had a lovely sense of humour and I liked him enormously, but I had no inkling then of the important role he would later play in my life.

At about this time too I grabbed the chance to visit Elstree Studios and, even quicker, the invitation to appear in an Old Mother Riley film with Arthur Lucan and his wife, the intimidating Kitty O'Shea. I can't quite remember, but I think I played one of a group of nauseating schoolgirls. To do this I had to become a member of Equity, the actors' union. It was relatively easy in those days, but that card I acquired so casually then has served me well ever since. I had it made out in a different name. Feeling hampered by the 'Lady' and not mad about the 'Boyle' bit, I wrote and asked Richard to suggest a name for me. He replied: 'Why not use another of mine? I sit in the House of Lords as Baron Carleton – Catherine Carleton sounds rather nice, and you don't have to use the title.'

So as Catherine Carleton I became a member of Equity.

A Wife Alone

In the spring of 1948 my mother wrote to say that she and her husband had parted and that she was off to see her ever-faithful lawyer, Pecorella, in Rome. She was also suggested, as she was going to stay with friends we all knew, that Anne and I should join her there for a fortnight's holiday. We jumped at the idea.

Then, thinking it over, I began to get all uptight about going back to Italy. Even though Rome was at a safe distance from both Turin and Rapallo, I began waking up in the middle of the night screaming because of nightmares about being caught in a dense maze with all exits blocked by my father. Each night I planned to tell Anne that I couldn't face the trip, and each morning I told myself instead that I was being quite ridiculous. And, of course, we set off as happy as two sandbirds.

Years later when we were laughing over some press shots taken of us on the steps of the plane, we counted that, from top to toe, I was wearing no less than twelve colours – few of them blended and most of them clashed. When I asked Anne why she hadn't toned me down before we left, 'You looked so happy, I didn't like to hurt your feelings,' was her reply.

Once there I found it wonderful to be back in Italy. My love for what I've always considered to be 'my country' was as strong as ever, and so many things had happened to me in the two years I'd been away that my fear of my father had faded.

I went back to see everyone at the Sacred Heart, and with great enthusiasm picked up the threads with lots of schoolfriends. One of the first people I telephoned when I got to Rome was my childhood sweetheart, Orazio Blanc. Unfortunately, he wasn't in Turin when I rang and when he called me back, Anne and I were due to leave Italy the next day; but at least we had got in touch again, and we've kept in touch ever since. I've always clung to his friendship – the only permanent and lasting thing of my turbulent youth.

There were moments when I wondered whether I wouldn't be happier living in Italy again, but that was probably a touch of 'the grass is greener on the other side'. I certainly felt very content – perhaps the word is 'safe' – when Anne and I boarded the plane again for London.

One of the people I'd met again in Rome was Blanca Welter, who was by this time calling herself Linda Christian and was married to Tyrone Power. They were planning to come and live in London for a while as Ty was going to star on stage in *Mister Roberts*. The play was a great success, and the Powers became an active and popular part of the London scene in the late forties and early fifties. They rented a lovely flat high above Park Lane, and entertained lavishly and non-stop. It was a great thrill to be included on their 'regular' guest list, because I was still very star-struck.

Linda had fined down tremendously since our school days at Poggio and become incredibly glamorous, and Ty, of course, was one of the best-looking men I had ever seen; but I rather took them for granted as 'old friends' whereas when Gloria Swanson, Judy Garland, Michael Rennie, Binnie Barnes, Ray Milland, Jack Hawkins and many other famous stars appeared at various parties, I became ridiculously self-conscious and shy. This wasn't helped by my acute shortage of clothes for the occasions, particularly in comparison with the lovely things everyone else was wearing. I always had to arrive with my one and only cloth coat covering my one and only evening dress, and never for a moment did it occur to me that being 'Lady Boyle' might have helped to carry me through. I'd just sit and watch Gloria Swanson or Judy Garland sweep in, spreading their sparkling charisma. Miss Swanson was already on her health kick and an excellent advertisement for what she practised and preached.

Stephen Ward, the acknowledged scapegoat of the Profumo

scandal, was one of Linda's many satellites. He was a good-looking, rather unobtrusive young man who, when he was in the mood, made excellent lightning sketches of other guests.

I think I was always a bit of a puzzlement to Linda: not only did she get angry with me for what she called my 'little flower in the corner act', which she knew was basically and completely out of character, but above all she couldn't make out why, with Richard so far away, I wasn't making the most of being alone. Having introduced me in vain to a string of suitable studs, she got very frustrated and decided that I really wasn't worth bothering about. Luckily, before she threw in the sponge, she invited me to a girls' lunch with Doreen Hawkins and Mal Milland, and the memory of that meal with those two smart, amusing women is still a very pleasant one of those early days in London. But, would you believe it, even then I didn't have the courage to put all the questions I'd planned to ask about their husbands! How often, and in how many different circumstances, do we wish we had in our youth the experience which only age brings.

Being in that Old Mother Riley film must have gone to my head because the 'Windsor affair' came next. On the set one day the talk was about 'reps': how important it was to get into rep; what a lot of good rep could do for one; which rep was better than another and why, etc. etc. I finally plucked up courage and asked a girl what this 'rep' was! Looking at me with disdain and pity, she snorted 'A repertory theatre, of course,' and never addressed another word to me. But at least I had an answer. The next step was obviously to get into a rep. The consensus of opinion seemed to be that John Counsell owned and ran one of the very best in England; it was at Windsor. Set in the shadow of the Castle, the Theatre Royal was often visited by members of the Royal Family, and John with his wife, Mary Kerridge, have become over the years an important part of British theatrical history.

Anyway, I had the cheek to write and ask Mr Counsell for an interview. To my delight he agreed to see me, and I set off for Windsor dolled up to the nines. I wore my one and only suit, the sheerest nylon stockings I couldn't afford and a pair of very high heels. I could hardly teeter the short distance from Windsor Station to the theatre. Mr Counsell kept me waiting only a few moments, then I was called up to his office. A large room with a desk near the window, it looked out over Windsor High Street, and I could see that we were right under the castle ramparts.

John had a kind face and he beamed benignly at me as he asked me to sit down. He said he was casting the Christmas pantomime and, as I had applied for a job, he wondered if I could tell him what theatrical background I'd had.

I gulped. I hadn't really worked out what I was going to say, but as I never had a good enough memory to tell lies, I planned to stick vaguely to facts.

'Well, I'm just starting,' I heard myself say.

'Have you had any training?' I looked blank. He went on. 'Do you dance?'

'Oh, yes!' said I, brightly thinking of the gavottes, minuets and polkas I'd whirled into at Valsalice.

'Where did you learn?'

'Oh, my stepmother had a niece who practised with some ballerinas, then she taught me.'

'Where was this?'

'In Italy.'

Mr Counsell rubbed his nose thoughtfully, and decided to change his tack. 'Do you sing?'

'I haven't actually had my voice trained, but my mother has a nice voice, so has my father. My stepmother too, so I try and sing.' A slight pause.

'Have you ever acted?'

'Don't we girls always act?' I grinned – very proud of that one, I was.

'I mean have you ever been in a film? Have you ever acted on the stage?' Was he becoming just a little testy?

'Oh, yes, I've just been on [that sounded right] an Old Mother Riley film, and of course I've been to the cinema an awful lot, and seen a great many plays since I've been in London.'

There was a long pause. 'Where did you say you came from?'

'Italy.'

'Oh, yes.' I felt that by now Mr Counsell was slightly bemused.

'You're rather tall, aren't you?' Oh, horrors, he was trying to put me off.

'Only five feet, six inches and I'm slim.' I tried to slide down in my chair.

'Yes, I can see you have a good figure.'

'Oh, *please*, Mr Counsell, won't you let me try?' I couldn't let him turn me down after all this.

He smiled. 'Well, there's our choreographer, Bice Bellairs. I'll have to ask her if she'll take you into the chorus.'

He pushed a buzzer. Could Miss Bellairs please come to his office. I held my breath. The door opened and a dark-haired woman with a swinging walk, full of health and vitality, bounced into the room. With a wide toothy grin and friendly eyes, she held out a firm hand to me. I felt her look me over.

'I was wondering, Bice,' John said hesitatingly, 'whether you'd be prepared to take Catherine on in the chorus?'

Bice looked at me again, back at John, and suddenly I was being told that rehearsals started next morning punctually at nine o'clock. Once back on the train it suddenly hit me. I was going to appear on a professional stage, dancing in a real live professional chorus line. I just couldn't take it in. My thoughts flew to my father, but I called them back at once. He would certainly not have shared my excitement. But Anne did; she was wonderful. We, or rather I, chatted on all night about this, my first step to fame and fortune.

It was a quarter to nine when I walked into the rehearsal room the next morning. Most of the girls were already there. I looked at them and my heart sank. Each one was clad in variations of a leotard and tights, and they all wore flat ballet pumps. A few of them were limbering up, while others were chatting, but they all turned as I came in. I smiled. They smiled back, and one said, 'Our dressing-room is down the corridor – you can change there.'

Change? Good heavens! I hadn't thought about that. I had on the same things I'd worn the day before, including a hat. As the skirt was flared I had thought I could dance in it. I felt the blood rushing to my cheeks, and had to bluff.

'How stupid of me. I forgot to bring my other things.' I took off

my hat – it felt so silly. Then I peeled off my gloves – they felt unnecessary; I put them on the window-sill.

'Well, I'll take off my jacket and I'll just have to dance in my stock-
inged feet, won't I?' I burbled away to hide my embarrassment. I
shook off my shoes, took a few steps forward and slid on the wooden
floor.

'Oh, dear. Do you think I should take off my stockings too?'

'You'll get an awful lot of splinters in your feet if you do,' said
one girl, who looked particularly sympathetic to my plight. She came
closer to me. 'Haven't you ever been to a rehearsal before?'

'I'm afraid not.' I felt awfully near tears.

'But you can dance?'

'Well, yes, but ... I have a feeling it's not the kind of dancing
you do.'

There was a snigger from the other girls, but it wasn't unfriendly.
At that point Bice Bellairs breezed in and clapped her hands.

'Right girls. We're all here so let's get started.' With that everyone
seemed to fall into three straight rows. Bice then caught sight of me
doing my best to merge with the scenery. She looked slightly surprised, so again I took the lead.

'Miss Bellairs, I'm so sorry I came without the right clothes – I
think I'll have to leave.'

'No, no,' she reassured me,' it doesn't matter at all – let's see how
you get on.'

For those of you who have never attended the first rehearsal of
professional dancers, let me tell you that it is an awe-inspiring experience for the uninitiated, and this particular morning was no exception. Bice Bellairs went into the first steps of a routine. She stopped.
The dancers immediately followed them accurately. They stopped.
She started again. And the process was repeated three of four times.

'Right, let's take it from the top with music,' she said.

'Rolling round the world, looking for a rainbow' – the tune was
catchy and within seconds the girls seemed to be foot-perfect, ready
to go on. And me? Well, I was still struggling in the back row trying
to get the first few steps sorted out – and I had already got splinters
in my feet. I felt more like a disjointed elephant than a would-be
dancer, but I was determined to learn – in fact I was concentrating

so hard I didn't even notice that all the others had stopped dancing. When I did, I was so confused and embarrassed I blurted out, 'Oh, please may I resign. I'm wasting everyone's time.'

There was a split-second silence, then a loud guffaw and Miss Bellairs announced, 'You're not going anywhere, I'm keeping you in for the laughs.'

That wasn't quite how I'd planned it, but this was how I got into the pantomime *Dick Whittington* at the Theatre Royal, Windsor. It was, in fact, a vintage year: Geraldine McEwen played Dick's cat, Patrick Cargill was a wicked alderman, Paul Scofield was King Rat, and I fell madly in love with Idle Jack, played by Victor Adams. I was paid the princely sum of £5 a week and enjoyed every minute of the experience.

I think everyone else on the stage regarded me as an occupational hazard and tolerated me as an enthusiastic amateur. With the best will in the world I never did manage to be where I was meant to be at any given moment, or in the same place for two performances running. All the same I pranced around in my three-quarter-length tutu, tore enthusiastically into Khachaturian's 'Sabre Dance', clad only in veils, and, what's more, I did a most individual daily version of the hornpipe, wearing a sailor cap, shirt and shorts. The only saving grace was that even if my steps were rarely accurate, they were always in time to the music.

Soon after the pantomime closed at Windsor, a letter arrived from Richard saying that two months later he'd be back in England for good. He suggested that I look for a flat and sounded very happy that we would be able to settle down to normal married life at last. I was pleased with this news too. But living with Anne for the past months and being a sort of married/bachelor girl had been extremely pleasant. I couldn't help wondering whether, or perhaps just how much, we might have changed towards each other. The early twenties are such fast-developing years, and even when living together, young marrieds can so easily grow apart. But I dismissed these thoughts, and set out to find a flat.

Finding a flat on a Captain's pay and little else was no easy task. Luckily I had my 'life-savers' – the Kerrs stepped in and solved the problem, this time through Toinon de Bellaigue. The Vicomtesse de Bellaigue is Belgian, an enchanting woman, and she too was a member of the Royal Household – she was French tutor to the Princesses Elizabeth and Margaret. Luckily Toinon wanted to leave her flat in Culford Gardens and, as she had a great deal of understanding, she and I came to a satisfactory arrangement. She only made one stipulation: 'I have a daily called Joan. She is such a nice person and I promised I would only let the flat go to someone who would agree to take her on too.' Now, thirty odd years later, Joan is still with me.

Richard came back to a very warm welcome. He approved of the flat, and when he started work at Regimental headquarters in Birdcage Walk, we both felt that this was what domestic bliss was all about.

To begin with, there was just the two of us living there. Of course, Joan came three morning a week for the princely sum of 5/- (25p), and I couldn't abandon Doris, who'd been such a treasure to Anne and me, so she came and did the washing and ironing. There was also Richard's batman, who was supposed to polish his shoes and boots and look after his uniforms, but he seemed to spend a lot of his time chain-smoking and consuming inordinate quantities of eggs and chips which I could ill afford to provide.

In the evenings when we were at home, Richard and I would take it in turn to cook, and when we went out it was on a motorbike. I loved riding pillion and Richard was a wizard of a driver. One hair-raising trip took us on a black, rainy night from London to Basingstoke without the benefit of a headlight. After a four-hour nightmare ride, thanks to Richard's expertise, two drowned rats arrived safely at Ashe Park for the weekend. The next day the sun was shining so, from a battered old trunk in a ramshackle shed, he and I extracted his gorgeous ermine-trimmed peer's robes. Then, bedecked and complete with coronets, we pranced around the orchard under the baleful gaze of a few Jersey cows.

I also relish memories of raised eyebrows at embassies as we clambered off the motorbike and unclipped our trouser legs and skirt before sailing into the formalities of the evening – at least it was cheaper than the taxis we couldn't afford.

It's odd how, even nowadays, many people assume that money automatically goes hand in hand with a title. I certainly learned that being both Lady Boyle and poor could be a difficult combination – wherever I went I was offered credit: 'Oh, please, Lady Boyle, don't dream of paying now. I'll put it on your account.' And there I was, always bleating, 'No, no, please let me pay cash. I'd far rather.' And so would my bank manager, I thought.

It was partly because of all this that I decided to start modelling in earnest. I plucked up courage and went to see Jean Bell. She was at the top of the tree as an agent, and I was told that she was very selective about whom she chose to represent. My knees were trembling as I climbed the stairs to her office near Chelsea Town Hall. It didn't help to find her walls covered with pictures of coolly-confident, super-sophisticated lovelies in beautiful clothes. Apologetically I said that I was afraid all my clothes were wrong, and Miss Bell readily agreed. Outspoken, tough, chic but, I discovered, with a heart of gold, Jean Bell took me under her wing. She told me at once to lose weight, not heart, and packed me off to Dr Goller, with whom I shed a stone-and-a-half in record time. I got down to 8 stone 8 lbs, but had to battle to keep there. Back to Jean, who instilled a little clothes sense into me, then sent me to have a mass of pictures taken by Peter Clark and Alan Boyd. Their studios just off Pont Street were a hub of fun and gossip, as well as very hard work. Armed with my first professional photographs, Jean sent me off on an endless trek to advertising agencies and other photographic studios to peddle myself.

I lost count how many times I was turned down for jobs. Either my face was too chubby or my bosom too big, or I was too blonde when they wanted a brunette, or not blonde enough when they wanted a blonde. At the beginning the only people who seemed willing to employ me were those who wanted to use my title. Michael Lewis, for instance, signed both society queen Mrs Gerald Legge and me to extol the beauties of his range of blouses; and Pond's paid me some precious pennies to recommend their creams – which, coincidentally, I did use. But all this was pretty disheartening and hardly likely to boost my confidence.

One of my first steps in modelling led me to Simone Mirman.

Simone and Serge Mirman, both cleverly and charmingly French, already had their house at Chesham Place, and Simone, a brilliant milliner, was at the start of her very successful career. I was delighted that she chose me to wear one of her most spectacular ostrich-feather-trimmed hats for a show. That photograph was published every where, even across the Channel, and although Simone claims it gave her precious publicity, it certainly established me as a 'hat model'.

Although I was, in fact, quite slim, I always seemed to photograph plump. This was probably because I was rounded – *fausse maigre* as the French so aptly put it – so Jean felt I might be happier as a manne-quin. How right she was. I really found my feet, as it were, on the catwalk. But even these jobs didn't come fast and furious to begin with. Although I called myself Catherine Carleton, a lot of people knew I was Lady Boyle and this seemed to make them want to 'take me down a peg or two'. The result was that if the dressing-room was overcrowded I was the girl they shoved into the corridor to dress. If fittings were running late I was the one they kept the latest. Quite honestly they couldn't have picked a less deserving victim – all I wanted to do was to earn much-needed money.

I thoroughly enjoyed being a mannequin. I loved wearing the clothes, loved the contact I felt with the audience, smiling at them and having them smile back at me. But I was always getting into trouble over my grin. Remember that this was the era of the Glorious Goalen. Barbara Goalen glided aloofly along the ramps, often trailing thousand of pounds worth of furs along the floor behind her. A smile would never have sullied her lips and most of the other mannequins copied her. I found this quite impossible – and luckily there were others who didn't mind my exuberance, so Jean Bell was able to keep me pretty busy.

Mixed
Emotions

Every couple has to adjust to each other's idiosyncracies, and Richard and I weren't really doing too badly. Admittedly, he had to contend with a floating population of my friends from across the Channel who often spoke little or no English, as well as my tendency to collect various animals off the streets which I felt were in need of a home. We usually managed to find them homes with friends or relations, but we kept Nooky, the black-and-white Peke, given to me by Richard. I'd named him after a long-lost favourite dog in Italy, and was oblivious to the raised eyebrows his name caused. Then there was Zambra, the alsatian; I'd found him paw-raw and near to collapse in St James's Street and neither of us had had the heart to part with him.

Throughout our marriage, I had to contend with bits and pieces of clocks and/or cars which were strewn around the various rooms. After my first unappreciated attempts to tidy them up, I bleatingly agreed to let them adorn the place. My bleats only turned to roars if some obscure shape was left to 'bake' in the oven when I wanted to roast our dinner. Richard was in fact a most able do-it-yourself man, although his impetus sometimes flagged before the job was completed.

Then Mama came to stay. By tradition of course mothers-in-law should stay well away from their married offspring, but my mother was not only devoted to the two sons-in-law she was to have but was also loved deeply by them in return. By nature she was the original pourer of oil on troubled waters. So when she had extricated herself from her own marriage to her second husband, Richard and I welcomed her with open arms into our spare room half-way up the corridor.

It was while the three of us were living together that Patrick Boyle and Mama fell in love. This turn of events took everyone by joyful surprise, and we watched the courtship flourish from the wings.

It wasn't long though before the army interrupted our marriage again. This time Richard was sent off to West Africa, to be ADC to General Brocas-Burrows, so I was glad to have Mama living in the flat with me.

Soon after this, however, I was asked to go to Paris to do some photographic work during the collections. By now I was modelling full-time and this invitation was a tremendous seal of approval, so I jumped at the chance. It also gave me my first taste of what really hard work is all about.

When I first heard I was going to Paris I was overjoyed. There is a magic about that city which sets me tingling. I always feel a thrill deep down inside when I wander along the Seine and pause on its bridges, whether it be in the clear cool light of dawn, or the pink-edged glow of twilight. If this has a little to do with my having been happy there, I think it owes more to the special majestic quality of the city itself. Paris could never be anything except a capital; a beautiful city, truly built for kings, that weaves its own particular spell.

On this trip I had booked into the Hotel Roblin. It was small, quiet and very reasonable in those days. I had a glorious flight over, and was treading so lightly on air I hardly needed a lift to get to my room. The porter opened the door, put down my suitcase and handed me my key. How wonderful, I thought. I rushed to the window; then something told me I wasn't quite alone. Slowly I turned – and stared. There on my bed, under a thick blanket of red roses and dead to the world in the deepest sleep, lay Orazio Blanc. A typically imaginative gesture this of Orazio's, and what a reunion it was after all those years.

We worked all hours. The photographers wanted to take as many pictures as they possibly could, and as the clothes had to be in the salons for the shows each afternoon, we started work literally at dawn and, with the odd hour off in the afternoon, went on working, often until midnight. Tempers became frayed with the pressure of it all, and eventually I would reel into bed worn out mentally and physically. The effort of wanting to do my best was exhausting. I was well aware that most of the other girls were not only better-looking than I was, but also had a great deal more experience, and none of them seemed to be hindered by an overblown bust like mine, which always photographed twice its size anyway.

It was a pity I had to work quite so hard during that week in Paris, but Orazio and I still found time to catch up with each other and confirm what we had found out as children – that we liked one another very much indeed. We had a lot of laughs; climbed to the top of the Eiffel Tower; went to Carroll's – the gay girls' club – because I wanted to hear Dany Dauberson sing. A gorgeous lesbian in beautifully-cut tails asked me to dance; Orazio spurred me on, whilst I held back like a blushing bride, and simpered: 'But I wouldn't know what to do.'

'I only asked you to dance, darling,' she replied.

We then went on to the equivalent club for the gay boys, but left that even faster, because Orazio didn't know what to do either!

Orazio followed me faithfully from studio to studio, and waited for me to finish work. He even gave me a huge emerald ring, which I threw into the Seine in a fit of pique when he told me he had dared to get married. He swore afterwards that it had been a fake. Who knows? His delightful wife Isa and I became firm friends a few years later but, then and there, Orazio and I were catching up and indulging in a glorious – albeit brief – spell of escapism.

The enforced separations did nothing at all for my marriage. Each time Richard and I were together again after the months apart, not only did we feel we had grown away from each other, but we had lost the ability to communicate. This made Richard go further into his shell; I instead erupted irritably at every opportunity. One day, when pushed to my limit by some triviality, no doubt, I grabbed a packet of frozen peas and crashed them down on poor Richard's head.

'Get cross, for God's sake, get angry,' I can still hear myself shriek. This behaviour was hardly conducive to encouraging someone of

Richard's nature to be more outgoing and, of course, the vicious circle set in worse for me too. This is what incompatibility is all about. Of course, there was no thought of divorce, but we both immersed ourselves more deeply in our own individual interests. He spent a lot of time away at Pirbright, whilst I took all the modelling jobs I could all over the place.

Then something did bring us together for a while. My father came on the scene.

It was a morning in mid-January 1950 when the telephone rang, and a quiet voice said, 'My name is Bernard Rickatson-Hatt,' he hesitated, and I thought what an extraordinary name – it was the kind of name you could only make up.

'Yes?' For some unknown reason I was cautious.

'I assume you are Lady Boyle?'

'Yes,' again.

'Well, I thought you might like to know – um – that your father is in London.' He paused, and I felt as if a boulder had hit me. I could not say a thing.

'Are you still there? It is just that I thought you might like to see him.'

How much did this man know about our relationship? Had my father put him up to this call? What should I do? All of a sudden my inside had snapped into a tight ball; the fear I thought I had forgotten gripped me. This was quite ridiculous. I was a grown-up married woman. I had to pull myself together.

I heard myself say, 'Well, Mr Rickatson-Hatt, it is very kind of you to have telephoned, perhaps you would come and have a drink one evening ...' He grabbed this suggestion mid-air and, at six p.m. that same day, was on the doorstep.

Bernard Rickatson-Hatt looked like his name. Small, slim, with thinning grey hair, he was immaculately dressed in black jacket and pin-stripe trousers. An oval pearl held his silver grey tie in place, and he used his monocle expertly. He had the studied tactful manner of someone who was used to finding himself in delicate situations, so I was not in the least surprised to learn that he had been an intimate friend of both the Simpsons throughout the Abdication. He told me that he had been editor-in-chief at Reuters, but in fact, when he came into my life, he was closely connected with the Bank of England. It was immediately obvious how useful he could be to my father. There must still have been a lot of unravelling of Godmother's money to be done in this country.

With drink in hand, he began, 'You have not seen your father for quite a while, I believe?'

'No, It must be over five years.'

'Then you do not know either of the two children?'

What? I had no idea he had even ever had one. Now I *was* curious. Apparently, since I had left Augusta had first produced a girl, Margherita, then a boy, Enrico. She then, poor woman, had undergone the usual ordeal that my father planned for the women in his life who displeased him, and had been despatched (I was quite sure with no justification whatsoever) to a place very like the Villa Bertalazona. It was now a Mademoiselle Anne Marie Tache who was ensconced by my father's side in Richmond, Surrey, in the obvious role of 'the children's governess'. This trip to England was planned to last a month or so, because now they all lived together in Lausanne.

All this was quite a lot to absorb in one fell swoop. My years in England had given me a protective padding against my past, and here I was suddenly plunged back into it again. By the time Mr Rickatson-Hatt left, I felt a black bag had been put over my head, but that all my nerve-ends were painfully exposed.

The next day, Richard and I drew up outside a small house in Robin Hood Lane, Richmond, and there in front of us – I couldn't believe my eyes – was our old Rolls Royce. Good heavens. It must have been fifteen years old, but there it was, still gleaming with pride, and they had obviously driven over from Lausanne in it. It brought back so many memories and, if I had dared to, I would have turned tail and fled. Instead, clutching Richard's arm, I rang the bell and waited. At last the door opened, and everything happened at once. Two small children tugged at my clothes calling 'Caterinella, Caterinella'; a woman dived under our legs and retrieved a Peke puppy.

My father looked even larger than I remembered him, and he had put on weight. He was shaking hands with Richard, then Richard was shaking hands with a blonde, then ... the moment I had dreaded

– my father and I came face to face. Our eyes met. There was a total hush. I felt tears well up, and watched his eyes fill too; we leant slightly towards each other; and suddenly I was enveloped in the tightest of bear hugs, and we were both sobbing loudly. What a crazy scene. It lasted seconds, then we drew away from each other, slightly embarrassed. I heard him say, 'This is Anne Marie Tache.' As our two hands met, I felt the atmosphere grow cool. Whereas I had always felt there was an ebullient warmth about Augusta, from that very first moment I knew there was steel in the heart of this cold, efficient Swiss.

When the first shock of our meeting was over, I looked around me. This small drawing-room in a suburban, semi-detached house seemed such an incongruous setting for the large figure of my father. It made me feel claustrophobic, and I wondered how and why on earth he had decided to stay here of all places. He murmured some-thing about the country being good for the children, but as we were only yards off the busy main road I could not see the logic of this.

After about an hour of rather stilted conversation, during which I discovered that Margherita, a lively brunette of three-and-a-half, could do nothing right in Papa's and Anne Marie's eyes, and Enrico, a blond live wire of two, could do nothing wrong, Richard and I took our leave. As we reached the door, my father embraced us both fondly and pressed a flimsy white five-pound note into Richard's hand. 'Please give yourselves a little treat,' he said. I felt as though we had been tipped, but did not like to refuse. As we drove back to London, I leant back in a total daze.

Although I kept saying to myself that having my father in England could not possibly affect my life, the mere fact that he was here made me feel unsettled. For instance, it had been ages since a lawyer had crossed our paths professionally, but as soon as Papa turned up, sure enough, so did a lawyer. His name was Elio Nissim. My father had apparently helped him when there had been the purge of Jews in Italy. I had always liked Elio, but I never understood why my father had to have a 'legal adviser' forever at his beck and call.

Even though Richard and I were hard up, we were determined not to get involved financially with Papa. I was quite sure it was wiser to accept with grace the odd £5 note he handed over to us with a great flourish from time to time, and leave it at that. From bitter experience, I knew that close encounters of any kind could only spell trouble. The danger signals flashed brightly to prove my point when, one day, Richard and I offered to have the two children to stay the night so that Papa and Anne Marie could go to a theatre and dine afterwards. Not only was the suggestion turned down with what I considered to be unnecessary abruptness, but the very next morning I was summoned to Dottore Nissim's office and 'warned' that I had better not try to kidnap or alienate the youngsters from Papa in any way. If I did, I would land myself in very serious trouble.

'The man is mad,' was Richard's comment. 'It's a struggle to keep ourselves, let alone two kids!'

After that incident, we decided to steer clear of the lot of them. I felt safer. I felt safer still when Papa telephoned to say they were leaving the next day. Our enthusiastic goodbyes were tinged with relief as we watched them set off, piled high, waving feverishly and complete with the Peke, Oong Lou, in the Rolls.

Richard and I had definitely been drawn closer together during my father's stay in England. He had not only had a glimpse of this 'larger than life' character I had often tried, in vain, to describe, but had also seen Papa's draining effect on me. As for me, I had appreciated Richard's protective attitude tremendously, and we both renewed our efforts to be happy together. We stayed with friends at week-ends; we had people in for quiet dinners; we genuinely tried to share each other's interests. But our basic incompatibilities inevitably surfaced, and after a while, very sadly, we grew further and further apart again.

As if to hammer the wedge between us a bit further, a letter arrived one morning from *Vogue*. It was, in fact, from Rosemary Cooper, the editor of *Vogue Beauty Book*. She wrote that she was organizing some fashion shows in Australia. They were to be held in collaboration with David Jones Stores in Sydney and Adelaide, and with Myers Emporium in Melbourne. She was taking along a photographer, Anthony Denney, and four model girls and she wondered whether I would like to be one of them.

It sounded wonderful. I couldn't believe my eyes, and read the letter all over again. But – of course – I would have to talk it over with Richard. What had she said ... ? 'I am afraid we would be away for about two months.' Oh what *was* I going to do? It would be terribly selfish to up and go like that, but at the same time I knew Richard was not the kind of person who would want to stand in my way. It was the most incredible opportunity to see the world. Only I could decide one way or the other; Rosemary had given me ten days before she wanted an answer.

Mama was due back from the country any day, so I decided to wait and say nothing to anybody until I could talk the whole thing over with her. Unfortunately she arrived home just about the same time as I was expecting a modelling friend, Joy Galloway, and her husband to have a drink. They were bringing along a friend with whom they were going to dine afterwards. So, as I was anxious to get talking to Mama, I scribbled a note to Joy, saying something to the effect that I had had to go out unexpectedly. But just as I was sneaking out to stick it on the door, I heard voices, and Joy, John and their friend appeared at the top of the stairs.

'Well hello! You were impatient to see us!'

I crumpled the note behind my back. 'No more than you to see me! You're so punctual.' Laughing and joking we all tumbled into the flat. Then I heard Joy say, 'This is Greville Baylis.'

'It is very kind of you to let me come along.' The voice was deep velvet. I turned round and ... ! Now what on earth can I say without sounding corny? Nothing – because the honest truth was that Greville was tall, dark and handsome, and we fell in love, at first sight.

As soon as they left, I ran into Mama's room, and all I could say was, 'Oh darling, I have just met the man I shall marry.' I will never forget either her expression, or my own wonderful feeling. Later that evening the telephone rang. It was Greville and he said he had told Joy and John more or less what I had told Mama.

The next day we had lunch together. He mentioned that he was married, but separated from his wife. He asked me about Richard, and I talked about going to Australia. At the end of the week, I telephoned Rosemary Cooper to say I would love to join her team.

I did not need anyone to tell me that, at that particular moment, a chance to have two months away from everything and everybody could only be a godsend.

Far-away Places

On a cold grey January morning, my spirits were very high as I stepped on to the plane. The quintet of 'model girls', as we were called then (presumably to distinguish us from artists' models), was made up of Jean Dawnay, Laura Parnell, Della Oake, Rosemary Cooper and myself. Jean Dawnay was Christian Dior's favourite model at the time – she is now Princess George Galitzine, and still just as pretty. Laura Parnell, a lovely Italian brunette (funny that there should be two Italians representing Britain!), had a delicious sense of humour and wore clothes with inimitable Latin chic. Then there was Della Oake – very tall, incredibly willowy, with the largest eyes I've ever seen; although not strictly a beauty, she was stunningly good-looking, but her sweet smile belied an astringent character. To complete the group there was Rosemary Cooper and Anthony Denney, our official photographer, who was a darling.

It's funny how travelling by air seemed less hurried in the early fifties – there was even time for a bus tour round Rome while the plane was refuelling. Although we only saw a waiting-room and sipped coffee in Cairo because it was already dark, I remember our overnight stay in Basra as being very leisurely. I even had seven hours sleep in the then Transit Hotel – plenty of time to catch a cold as a result of my first introduction to air-conditioning – and there was no hurry next morning when Anthony took photographs of Jean and me on the shores of the Euphrates.

It was in Sri Lanka (Ceylon as it was then called) that an official gazed at my passport, then up at me and beamed 'Ah, vice-countess! Welcome!' and, of course, a 'vice-countess' I remained. Sri Lanka gave me my first taste for the tropics, which I've never lost: that wall of humid heat that hits you as you step onto the tarmac; the heady scent of frangipani flowers, the hibiscus, jacarandas and bougainvillaea; the colourful clothes of the locals, especially the children; the waving, whispering palms cooling the air; the tepid Indian Ocean lapping lazily on the soft platinum sand.

We were driven along the coast to the Mount Lavinia Hotel for breakfast, where the lime juice lifted the taste of my first pawpaw, and tiny humming-birds shared my sugar-bowl. Oh! yes, this place was made for lovers, and even after only a few hours I was loathe to leave Sri Lanka. Luckily, Laura and I had already planned to linger a while on our way back from Australia.

On the seven-and-a-half-hour next leg of our journey to Singapore, I discovered that although flying didn't swell my feet and ankles as it did the rest of our party, it made my skin parchment dry and my eyes badly bloodshot, so ever since then I've always carried salt-water eye-drops to keep my eyes 'liquid' during the actual flight, and Blue Eye Dew to re-whiten the whites before landing. What's more, I get through a small jar of nourishing cream (moisturiser is too mild), patting it in around my eyes, mouth and neck as I go – the skin laps it up so fast that even if my neighbour is male, he doesn't notice, let alone take fright.

Singapore was stiflingly hot, although we arrived late at night. We were welcomed effusively and given fans made of scented wood and freshly picked gardenias. Then we were driven, more dead than alive, to Raffles Hotel. Named after Singapore's founder and great benefactor, Sir Stamford Raffles, this hotel is unique. Even now, in the eighties and despite being virtually hemmed in by skyscrapers, this rambling two-storey building retains its magic with so many memories of days gone by. But in 1952, of course, it was far less sophisticated. Air-conditioning had yet to be taken for granted and that night, after our long journey, we lay naked and panting on our beds below fans with enormous blades which rotated noisily on the ceiling.

Many of the bedrooms still open onto the wooden verandahs

which run, uninterruptedly, along the building on both floors. That first night, way back in 1952, when I went into Raffles, I felt just as I did when I returned there in the late 70s – that I'd stepped into the middle of a Somerset Maugham story.

It wasn't until many years later that I began to really know and love Singapore, but amongst my first fleeting memories is one of fiddling with high fashion-shoes outside innumerable temples (green to Far Eastern customs, we didn't know that shoes are not allowed inside). We dined with the Chinese Tiger Balm millionaire A.W. Boon Haw (Tiger Balm being the all-purpose pain-killer of the East). He kept crocodiles as pets and let their offspring scuttle around the verandah, and his prized possession was an outsize American fridgidaire, which he'd placed in the centre of the drawing-room. We gazed at his collection of glorious jade objects through the glass doors of hideous Victorian cabinets. I remember, too, sampling birds'-nest soup and eating satay – flaked meat or chicken rolled round slim sticks and dipped in delicious peanut sauce.

After Singapore, there was a brief stop in Djakarta; then finally, four days after leaving London, we landed in Australia – Darwin to be exact. We stepped into a moonlit Turkish bath, and stayed just long enough to taste our first large Australian steak and gawp at the buildings around the airport – they were built high up on wooden stilts, presumably out of the way of tropical floods. Our last lap, from Darwin to Sydney, took us into brilliant 7 a.m. sunshine to face a battery of press photographers and newsreel cameras. None of us expected this blast of instant fame which was to follow us throughout the tour.

Four top Australian models joined our team in Sydney. Friendly, good-looking girls, they were Judy Barraclough, Norma Geneave, Karen Scammell and Bambi Shmith. Bambi, so-called because of her gazelle-like looks, was still married to Australian photographer Athol Shmith, and her marriage to the Earl of Harewood was still many years away.

Looking back and trying to be objective I still think the shows themselves had great style. The audience sat at small clusters of tables in the restaurants, and the catwalks were built high, and wound round them. We ran the gamut of British fashion, from furs, through tweeds, silks, satins and chiffons and ended with a magnificent, full, Court presentation dress designed by Frederick Starke, in multiple layers of fine white lace, complete with train. I wore this with tiara, ostrich-feather head-dress, near shoulder-length white kid gloves and carried a flowing ostrich-feather fan. This outfit brought the show to a spectacular close, and how I loved wearing it, though I could hardly breathe, pulled into a twenty-three-inch waist. I nearly brought the house down on the very first night: I dipped into the lowest Court curtsey, and as I came up, both rhinestone shoulder-straps snapped. There was a second's stunned silence, then the audience roared its appreciation as my highly-colourful reaction was amplified by the live microphone.

Although I was happy, those two months were very strenuous. We worked far harder than we played. Late nights were out, and during the day, apart from the two shows, we were busy with press and radio interviews (no TV in those dark ages), photographic sessions and general 'public relations'.

Melbourne greeted us as enthusiastically as Sydney had done. It struck us that the bustling, throbbing vitality of Sydney was replaced in Melbourne by a nearly tangible respectability and a calmer pace of life. I also remember that Melbourne had none of the usual poorer areas that other towns seem to have on the way from the airport. All the houses and roads appeared clean and well-maintained and there were masses of flowering bushes on the roadside.

Our arrival in Melbourne coincided with that of the accepted star model girl of all time, Barbara Goalen; she, too, was working with a fashion house. Not only can she wear a sack and stamp it 'High Fashion' and has the smallest, neatest feet with the highest instep I've ever seen, but she is also one of the friendliest people and has a lovely sense of fun. She is the perfect proof that a good-looking woman can only gain by being pleasant.

It was in Melbourne that we heard the news that King George VI had died in his sleep, and that the young Princess Elizabeth was Queen. The city itself seemed stunned, and the strong bond of the Royal Family to the Commonwealth struck home emotionally when traffic, police and pedestrians were petrified in a two-minute silence a few days later.

In Adelaide, when the tour was nearly over, Rosemary and I were having a late-night mull over the past weeks. We'd all got on remarkably well and I said so.

'Yes, hasn't it been wonderful,' agreed Rosemary. 'I'm so glad I didn't listen to gossip about you.'

Seeing I looked bewildered she went on: 'I couldn't have done much about it, but I must admit I was a bit worried about bringing you.'

Apparently, shortly before we left London, someone – a woman – had taken the trouble to go and see Rosemary and warn her that she'd be most unwise to include me on the team because I was ... 'a secret drinker', and ... 'a raving nymphomaniac – but only with waiters, you know'. What this female didn't know was that I'd already signed my contract, so Rosemary had been obliged to stick to it. And I, gloriously unaware of her misgivings, had had plenty of time to prove my innocence, albeit quite unconsciously. What price bitchery!

We left Australia with a feeling of great warmth for that country, loads of happy memories and plans to go back there one day – I still hope I shall. I had thrown myself into the Australian tour with both enthusiasm and relief. It was blatant escapism in one sense, as I'd left behind a situation I neither wanted, nor felt able, to face – and now that the two months were up I was no clearer in my mind. That instant attraction and strange 'permanency' I'd felt towards Greville hadn't decreased at all.

When I left London he'd got in touch with *Vogue* to check my schedule and this meant there had been a steady flow of letters from him. What's more there was a special 'welcome' telephone call when I got to each new town – and he always took into consideration the twelve-hour difference so as to catch me at a convenient 8 a.m. my time. We kept the tone between us light so, I told myself, there was no harm in 'keeping in touch'. It's so easy to kid yourself when you're half a world apart.

Once again I set what I felt was going to be a big problem to one side. Anyway there was the immediate excitement of our holiday to contend with. Della and Jean went off to New York, Rosemary and Anthony to New Zealand, and Laura and I planned to dawdle

ABOVE LEFT Our first holiday together: Greville and I in Montego Bay, Jamaica
ABOVE RIGHT Our wedding day in August 1955

Greville at his happiest

With Sugar Plum and Tai Tai

Promotional assignments: encouraging denture wearers (but my teeth are my own)
with Michael Whittaker on my right, a woman of many parts, and flying the flag
in an Ideal Home Exhibition kitchen

ABOVE Happy times in Kenya
ABOVE RIGHT Our last holiday together: Greville pats Girlie, after his accident, about ten days before he died

BELOW Alone in a crowd

ABOVE My father in a Russian *rubashka*
ABOVE RIGHT Enrico, my half-brother

BELOW My mother and her third husband, Patrick Boyle (now Lord Cork and Orrery)
BELOW RIGHT Margherita, my half-sister, with Barouf

ABOVE Me, Denis Lowson and Frank Longford at a fancy-dress ball
ABOVE RIGHT A recent portrait of me in stippled watercolour by W. P. Mundy

BELOW H.M. The Queen Mother with Peter and me on the eve of her seventy-ninth
birthday, at *The Mousetrap*

Peter and I on our way home after our wedding in Lausanne

our way back to England via Singapore, Ceylon and Bombay. It was too good a chance to miss.

In fact, from Singapore we also flew to Kuala Lumpur in a tiny plane, buffeted frighteningly by the quick storms which blow up suddenly in the Tropics. Laura's father-in-law lived in Kuala Lumpur and had invited us to stay for a weekend.

From Kuala Lumpur we flew to Ceylon. To our surprise, when we stepped out of the plane there, at the foot of the ramp was the local press, complete with cameras, to greet us. We had thought our posing days were over for a while, but, quite happily, we put back on our professional smiles. Then, suddenly, out of the corner of my eye I saw the white-clad figure of a man. I looked again. There, handsomely tanned, with shirt and trousers immaculately pressed, a casually-knotted yellow scarf around his neck, stood Greville Baylis. He smiled and waved. My heart missed a beat; my mind went blank. But Greville welcomed Laura and myself equally warmly – funnily enough her then husband, Charles Parnell, and he were old acquaintances. What's more, he made his appearance in Ceylon seem perfectly natural.

'Before the flat-racing season starts again in the spring,' he said, 'I always take a winter holiday. It's usually been in the West Indies, so I thought I'd have a change this year.'

I knew nothing about horse-racing but during the lunch we'd had together in London, Greville had told me he was mad about the sport; and his link with the West Indies came from his being ADC, just after the war, to the then Governor of Trinidad, Sir Bede Clifford. Later he'd taken over from Sir Edward Cunard as Sir Bede's private secretary, so Edward and various other friends in the West Indies had always invited him to stay. Apart from these few facts, though, this man was still a stranger. Yet there he was, far away from home, and so was I. The impact I'd felt at our first meeting, and his undeniable charisma, were not only stronger for me than ever, but never faded throughout our life together.

For the next two weeks the three of us explored Ceylon together. But there was one morning, when Laura baulked at a 5 a.m. rise, that we went off shark-fishing with some local fishermen. This wasn't our most romantic outing as we spent most of the day darting to opposite sides of the boat, to be violently and discreetly sick, and trying to pretend to each other that we were having a marvellous time. What we hadn't bargained for was the fisherman dropping anchor once we were out at sea; the combination of blazing heat, the slow incessant roll of the boat and the thudding blows on the heads of the unfortunate animals before they were dragged bloodily aboard, completely finished us off. We must have been on this trip for something like eight hours, but by the end of them, and through our mutually-confessed suffering, our friendship was cementing fast.

Laura was an easy, unobtrusive and tactful companion. There were her extra shopping and sightseeing expeditions with our driver, and those early siestas which left Greville and me to linger over our coffee. We had plenty of time to find out things about each other. Unfortunately, set down in black and white, certain facts were very worrying.

By his brief wartime marriage to Pat Maxwell Wiltshire, Greville had a son, Mark, who in 1952 was eight years old; and, though virtually separated, he was then still married to his second wife, Jean, who was some years older than him. Jean was one of the three half-American Garland oil heiresses who, between them, had already notched up nine husbands. Arthur Smith-Bingham and Sir Robert Throckmorton had preceded Greville and now, apparently, the atmosphere between Jean and himself was sulphuric. Like so many rich women, she was unable to shed husbands amicably.

For my part, despite my unorthodox background and because of my Catholic upbringing, I felt one just didn't shed them at all. If I hadn't been falling more in love with Greville each day, I don't suppose I would have worried much about his tangled matrimonial web. As it was I just knew I was going heart first into an impossible situation.

Presuming everything went according to Greville's intentions and he would eventually be free to re-marry, even if I did manage to get an annulment of my marriage to Richard, as a Catholic I would never be able to marry a once, let alone twice, divorced man. And what about Richard? Being with Greville in this casual, light-hearted way had already made me realize that there was a whole fund of untapped emotion in me. What I felt towards Richard was, and still is, a very genuine deep affection, but not the kind of love that moves mountains and without which one knows one will die.

All the same, the very last thing in the world I wanted to do was to hurt my husband. But would he be hurt? So often during our spasmodic marriage I'd said I feared I was bad for him. His clever scientific mind and somewhat ponderous personality was at times bewildered and upset by my Latin temperament. Wouldn't it then be a relief for him not to have me around? But then again, was this just wishful thinking? How many times in life does one reason things round 'logically' to suit oneself, and after all, one doesn't betray one's marriage vows for such inoffensive differences. No – this was ridiculous. More than that, I was being wickedly selfish at the very best. I had to pull myself together and regard this Ceylon holiday as a happy, innocent interlude.

So it was on this controlled emotional note that we flew from Colombo to Bombay. I'd always been intrigued by India and was determined to sublimate all other feelings into the excitement of seeing as much of Bombay and its surroundings as possible. Greville was going to fly straight back to England; Laura and I had a further fortnight to look forward to. But things didn't run according to plan. A few minutes after take-off, I looked at Greville and to my horror saw his brow heavily beaded with perspiration and his face tinged with green.

'It's a migraine, I'm afraid – I feel awful.' He didn't have to tell me, though I'd never seen a migraine before.

The sun was suddenly too bright – I pulled the blinds down over the portholes around us. I came back to find him groping in his brief-case for some Bufferin.

'They're the only pills that cut through the worst of the pain,' he said. Then he held up a bottle of menthol and suddenly splashed this stinging liquid into his open eyes. I yelped out in sympathy for him then, with one pain fighting the other, he just lay back exhausted. And I just lay back falling more in love with him, all my good intentions shattered to smithereens.

The cause of the migraines was a recent car crash in which he'd been a passenger: he'd been sound asleep, and was hurled through the windscreen against the back of a parked lorry. The poor man had been left on the side of the road for dead until someone saw him move and rushed him to a local hospital where a gaping wound in his badly-fractured skull was sewn up very neatly by a . . . gynaecologist.

When we reached Bombay, Greville still felt so wretched that he decided to cancel his flight to London and stay two days longer. These days flew and, when he did leave, I felt a painful void. Laura and I, however, found plenty to do. We bumped into Maureen O'Hara's husband, Will Price, whom we both knew vaguely, and he took us on locations to see an Indian technicolor epic being filmed at night.

During all this time, Greville kept in touch. He telephoned when he got home and suggested that Laura and I break our journey back so that he could fly to Rome and meet us. I persuaded him not to, although the temptation was tremendous. It was very difficult not to be carried along by his enthusiasm. It was also wonderful to know he was already so sure of his feelings, but just because of this, I didn't want to set a fuse alight. For one of the rare times in my life, and because I was fully aware that the outcome of our complicated state of affairs was vitally important for our happiness, I curbed my impulses.

Laura and I spent our last day in Bombay at Morvi Beach soaking up the sun, and I couldn't wait to board the plane back to Britain. By now I was prepared to tackle everything that lay ahead.

Stars and
Storms

We'd been away for nearly three months and it was spring when Laura and I landed at London Airport. Richard and Howard Kerr were there with a warm welcome; they could never have guessed the turmoil going on inside me. Anyway, they were full of the news that Mama had just married Patrick Boyle. A telegram telling me this had obviously missed me in Bombay, so all the details of this latest turn of events carried us over the first few awkward hours.

During the following weeks, I swung wildly to and fro in my feelings. I was totally convinced that Greville and I were two halves of a whole, but my religious beliefs, my feelings for Richard and my overall sense of guilt were tying me up in knots and I hadn't the slightest idea of how to unravel them. Next came my dramatic statement to Greville that we 'must never see each other again', with which he smilingly agreed. He knew full well it was hardly likely and by now he was prepared to bide his time.

It's odd – and I would have thought it in contradiction to my apparently extrovert character – but when life calls for serious decision, I always look inwards. I go to nobody but myself or into a church for the answers and now, faced by this most important of crossroads, I had to work things out alone, and pray.

Just about this time, the BBC producer, Richard Afton, who had been in touch with me once before, repeated his invitation: would I appear in the 'Beauty Spot' of his forthcoming show to be called 'Quite Contrary'? My first reaction was to refuse. I had gone back to full-time modelling and at any other time would have jumped at the chance – but now, in my muddled emotional state, I hadn't the heart to branch out in any way.

But Dickie Afton isn't Irish for nothing and his powers of persuasion are great. What's more I had a call from Greville and when I told him of this offer he immediately said: 'Darling, you must accept. Television is *the* thing of the future – you can get in on the ground floor.' I still hesitated – after all the show was still in its planning stage – and then Dickie triggered my pride: 'You'll only be on the screen for a minute. I don't know what you're making such a fuss about – nobody will remember you.' That did it! I agreed to be at Lime Grove Television Studios on the day of rehearsal.

In the early fifties the Television Centre in Wood Lane had yet to be built and only a few left-over programmes were still being done at Alexandra Palace (Ally Pally), so everything was happening at Lime Grove and Studio G was the largest studio there. By comparison to most of today's studios it was small – cramped in fact – and the lights were so low-slung we sweated under and were drained by the intensity of their heat. From time to time a big wooden door was flung open, and a noisy fan cranked into action to enable us to breathe. The shows were 'live', happening before your very eyes – fluffs, breakdowns and all. Recordings were very rare and astronomically expensive in those days.

It's even more surprising to think how many big names were made by the shows Richard Afton produced for BBC television. This small, dark man, with bright brown eyes behind horn-rimmed glasses, a stubby cigar stuck in an incongruous holder, had not only an enormous flair for picking new talent, but also the courage to back his judgement by putting it on the small screen. On 'Quite Contrary' alone, he launched female singers Joan Regan, Dolores Ventura, Mary O'Hara complete with harp (but long before she was widowed and retreated into a convent) and husky-voiced Ruby Murray. I shared one of my first days at Lime Grove with Ruby and, not knowing exactly who she was, when she croaked a friendly 'Hello', I said wasn't it lucky she didn't have to talk on the show. 'It's much worse, I'm afraid,' came her reply, 'I have to sing!'

The male singers included Carl Brisson, Michael Holliday and

Ronnie Hilton. There was Bert Weedon the guitarist, Violetta Elvin the ballet dancer, and Irene Handl and Pat Coombs came to stay after a comedy sketch they did in an early 'Quite Contrary'. The Television Toppers were also a Richard Afton creation: six blondes and six brunettes, all the same size, were auditioned and selected by Dickie personally. These girls danced through many a programme and their success spanned seventeen years. Incidentally, one of them, Gillian Creighton-Blair, became Mrs Afton.

There were lots of other people too who, though strictly borderline 'show business', were definitely good entertainment. Teasy Weasy for instance: already well-established as Raymond, a first class hairdresser and master-cutter before Vidal Sassoon came on the scene, he acquired his nickname by 'Teasy-Weasying' (as he put it) the curls on the models while he combed their hair out in front of the cameras. And the last surviving descendant of Casanova, a Baron Casanova himself, came to display his *cordon bleu* skills long before Fanny Cradock took over television kitchens.

Dickie Afton brought the first Miss World to television and that was way back in October 1955. He always had an eye for a good story, so when Donald Campbell broke one of his first world speed records and the news came through to the control room during an actual show, Dickie had a note handed on the studio floor to Donald's first wife, Dorothy, who was the compère that night. She read it and burst into happy tears for all to see.

When I appeared in that first 'Beauty Spot' (for a fee of five guineas) I wore full evening dress – Victor Stiebel lent me one made in a glorious shimmering gold brocade – and I sat in an enormous, ornately-gilded chair. Beside me there stood an equally ornate candelabra on a marble pedestal. Behind me there were heavily-draped velvet curtains, and to complete the picture a 'heavenly choir' (the Littlewood Songsters – who else?) softly sang *Lovely Lady*. All I was supposed to do was be motionless, and look demure and straight into camera as it came closer and closer. My stage fright was great, but my sense of the ridiculous even greater – at the very last moment I couldn't resist a wink at that impersonal-looking lens.

Two other people who saw the fun in my superglamorized

appearance were Eric Barker and Pearl Hackney. They had a TV series on at the time and in their show the following week, there was Pearl, sitting in a similar chair. Her dress was a dead ringer for mine, as was her hairstyle; but to bring things firmly down to earth, as the camera pulled out, it revealed Pearl holding a frying-pan full of sizzling sausages over ... the identical candelabra.

Dickie, far from being deterred, was tickled pink by such a reaction and the 'Beauty Spots' carried on. Anne, Duchess of Rutland and that outstanding good-looker, Fiona Campbell-Walter (Baroness Thyssen), were two of the many who sat in the hot seat.

As for me, after that first appearance, Dickie suggested that I should take over the introducing of the show. I was thrilled with the idea and that's how, for the next two years, 'Quite Contrary' became very much a part of my life. My fee, by the way, went up to a princely ten guineas.

Instant fame went with the kind of launching Richard Afton gave me on television in those days, and I really am a creation of that particular TV age. Not only were the numbers of viewers jumping from the hundreds of thousands into the millions, but the early fifties were also the vintage years of panel games. When you're playing a game, you usually reveal yourself as you really are; individuals, previously unknown, suddenly appeared in more and more homes and their impact was that of *personality* rather than performer. I've always jibbed at that 'television personality' label – but after all, according to the dictionary, to be a 'personality' is to have a 'distinctive personal character', and with no specific talent to help me along, I should, I suppose, be grateful for that.

Early on, I learnt that viewers react subjectively to anyone on the small screen. One night while playing 'The Name's The Same' with Frank Muir, Denis Norden and Brenda Bruce, I was more than usually lively and pretended to despair when I'd given the wrong answer. A few days later, I received two letters quoting this same incident. One said 'Dear Lady Boyle. The sooner you get off our screens the better – there is no room for someone like yourself who lacks all sense of humour and takes losing so very badly ...' The other went, 'Darling Katie. At last someone on our screens who bubbles with humour, and who plays games as they should be – just for the fun of them, never minding whether you win or lose...' Ever since then I've never pretended to be anything but natural – although, of course, we all have different lights and shades so I probably haven't always appeared the same.

Richard Afton swears it was the 'Quite Contrary' crew who first called me 'Katie', he says he even rousted them on the grounds (unfounded, of course) that Lady Boyle might object. But, according to my memory, I owe the tag to Frank Muir. Frank, knowing that I needed to earn my living, felt as I did that swanning around as 'Lady B' would be a handicap in show business. 'Just replace it with Katie,' he said. 'It rhymes, and with a bit of luck, in time people will drop the "Lady" and forget you've ever been one!'

It was soon after I'd settled into 'Quite Contrary' that Maurice Winnick came into my life. Maurice, who'd been a very successful dance-band leader, had recently branched out as an artists' agent. He had a clever tie-up with the American Goodson & Todman team who owned most of the popular panel games. This enabled him to virtually place his clients on them, whether the producer approved or not, so when he offered to be my agent I was delighted. Had I not been so inexperienced I might not have agreed with such glee to his taking 50% of all my earnings – even in these inflated days 10% or 15% are the more usually accepted terms.

But I have every reason to be grateful to Maurice Winnick. As 'Blankety Blank' and 'Give Us a Clue' are proving today, panel games will always be popular and in those days they were really the rage. Under the Goodson/Todman/Winnick banner I must have played most of them at some time or another – and all over the world. Apart from 'The Name's the Same', there was 'I've Got a Secret', 'Tell The Truth', 'Pick The Winner' – the full list would cover the page.

Contrary to a widely-held belief, I hardly ever appeared on 'What's My Line?' in England. In America, yes, and I did launch and play it regularly in Italy for several months. Over there it was called 'Che cosa fa il Signor X?' ('What does Mr X do?'), and I had some hair-raising experiences flying weekly, in all kinds of weather, to and from Milan. It was always on the tightest of schedules too, because the Italian show fell on a Tuesday and I had two others on

Monday and Wednesday back in England. It was after throwing family and friends into apoplexy by disappearing to Munich in a snowstorm instead of landing in a London peasouper, and leaving producer and team tearing their hair without me on a live transmission, that I gave up my weekly cross-Channel jaunts. They were certainly more hazardous than the transatlantic jetting of today.

Looking back on it, the notoriety which came with appearing on television was incredible, ludicrous and out of all proportion. Love you or loathe you, no one ignored you – particularly the press, thank goodness! It was their concentrated publicity during the first years, and very frequent mentions ever since (never, I must add, through a press agent), that established me so firmly as a 'name'. It really is thanks to the press that today, so many years later, even if people don't always know exactly what Katie Boyle does, the name still seems to ring a bell. In those days, the length of Barbara Kelly's earrings, Isobel Barnett's acute perception or Gilbert Harding's latest eruption could be guaranteed to make News (with a capital 'N').

Few people who loved to hate Gilbert Harding realized that he lived in continual physical discomfort. He and I made a number of personal appearances together. One evening in particular began early, with us emptying a large collection-box in a pub for the National Society for Mentally Handicapped Children. Then we were driven on to Bournemouth to an official dinner where we were guest speakers. As we went in, he growled 'For God's sake, Katie, if I nod off, wake me up ... somehow!'

I noticed that he was hardly drinking at all, but sure enough, half-way through the evening, I had to reach across to prod him awake. His actual speech was short and excellent, but he appeared to talk with difficulty. It was only when we set off back to London that I realized what a dreadful state he was in. The journey home was a nightmare. He used his asthma spray time and again, and eventually the driver had to stop. Together we heaved Gilbert out of the seat and sat him in the fresh air while we tried to revive this heavy man slumped between us.

Eventually, in the early hours of the morning, and very upset when we tried to persuade him that we should take him to hospital, he insisted that I leave him to his devoted chauffeur's care. Shortly after this experience I was hardly surprised, but nevertheless heart-broken, to hear that Gilbert Harding had collapsed and died at the entrance to Broadcasting House. How sad, but how appropriate, that his life should end there. He really was one of the greatest BBC personalities of all time.

If my public life was swimming along successfully, I was floundering badly over my private problems. A situation that had been very strained for me, and couldn't have been happy for Richard, now reached breaking-point. We sat and talked into the nights with deep sadness, and decided there was no point in dragging out something that would inevitably, eventually snap. Maybe this is why Richard and I have remained real friends with none of the bitter resentment associated with so many broken marriages. But even, or perhaps especially, when there is affection and no animosity, breaking away from someone is a very painful process. I don't believe, however, that I'm finding a sop for my conscience when I say I was convinced that to separate was the best solution for both of us. I think the years too have proved this to be so. As the Earl of Shannon, he is now a most successful international businessman in the research, architectural and engineering fields in which he showed such early promise, and is the father of three delightful children.

The actual packing and parting, of course, were horribly traumatic. Then there was the far-from-easy problem of where to live. I only had the money I was earning and I needed all the work I could get, so I couldn't take much time off to look for a new home. I settled for a bed-sitter in Sloane Avenue Mansions as a stop-gap – and it was just that: one room, a cupboard-sized kitchen and a tiny bathroom. With all my worldly goods crammed into this small space, it was dark and depressing and I got more and more despondent.

I was very anxious that Greville shouldn't get involved in my separation from Richard nor me in his from Jean, and I didn't want to burden my friends with all my troubles, so it was a desperately lonely period. The only person who came round regularly was Joan, my daily. Her job, apart from dusting down the suitcases, was non-existent so she became more and more my 'mate'. I think I'd have gone round the bend without her solid London common sense and unflagging loyalty.

There's no doubt about it though, in life when things just can't get worse they do seem to take a gradual turn for the better. My turn came in the elegant form of Hugh Wontner, a wonderful man, as astute in business as he is kind and good-looking. At that time he had yet to become London's Lord Mayor and 'Sir Hugh', but he was already Chairman of the Savoy Hotel and Managing Director of Claridges. He contacted me because he was planning to install a French hairdresser in the Savoy and wondered whether I'd like to act as a bilingual link in the enterprise. 'You can have a room on our top floor – in the "servants' quarters",' he laughed, 'and you can stay until you've sorted yourself out a bit.'

I jumped at the job. Not only was the thought of escaping from my rat-trap a great morale booster, but going to stay at the Savoy in my impecunious state appealed to my sense of the ridiculous!

From the eighth floor of the Savoy, the world looked a much friendlier place, and my large bedroom and bathroom were a peaceful haven through my emotional storms. My priority, however, was to find a more permanent place to live so as not to take advantage of Hugh Wontner's understanding help. And this is where Greville stepped in firmly. From that very moment he began to show me that protective, caring love which never failed me throughout the twenty-four years we were together.

He waved aside my objections about being seen together and soon found me a flat in Draycott Place. This I shared for a few months with the then fashion editor of *Queen* magazine, Anne Trehearne. Annie Pan, as everyone called her, was a great character, and very lovable. A platinum blonde with finely-chiselled features, she had a great heart, but was decidedly scatty and impractical. She once watched a paraffin-stove leak profusely over the drawing-room carpet and did nothing about it because, she said, 'I didn't quite know what to do.'

By now there was no doubt in either Greville's or my mind that one day we would marry, but it was one of those ambitions in life that have to be stored firmly in the subconscious because the present situation makes it quite impossible. It's strange, but making up my mind about something I want desperately, then setting it to one side, normally ensures that it will eventually happen. Of course, I'm always prepared to give it a personal prod as a reminder.

My dream of marrying Greville was a perfect case in point, and right then, there was no prodding I could do. The action was definitely in Jean's court. Her hostility towards Greville was quite unbelievable, and it wasn't long before she set detectives on our tail (not at all difficult, because with TV fame had come instant recognition wherever I went). It was grossly unfair because I hadn't known either Greville or Jean when they were living together, so had nothing to do with their break-up, and, in any case, Jean had walked out on Greville.

Then Jean went a step further and tried to enlist Richard's help. She suggested that he and she should join forces and put in a cross-petition for divorce against Greville and myself. Once again, though, Richard's understanding and kindness came up trumps. Not only did he turn her idea down point-blank, but he came to see me. 'Apart from anything else,' he said, 'I really do want you to be happy, so I intend to wait. If, after three years, you and Greville still love each other and want to get married, I'll divorce you quietly for desertion.'

A year had gone by. Jean's and Greville's lawyers were still at loggerheads and the winter weather was lousy when Greville telephoned from the country (he had a house at Copsale just outside Horsham). 'I've booked us on a flight to Jamaica, darling. Will next week suit you?' For me, never having been a women's libber, one of his most endearing traits was the way in which he took the reins. This reaction to all the strain and frustration of the past year was fabulous, and our first of many happy holidays in the West Indies was gloriously romantic.

The impact and brilliant beauty of the West Indies was stunning. They weren't overrun by tourists when I first came to know them. In the early fifties even the stamp-sized, palm-fringed Doctor's Cave Beach wasn't crowded; and Jamaicans, young and old alike, were friendly, relaxed, extrovert people who were forever smiling.

After the astringent cool of the Mediterranean I found the Caribbean was like a tepid bath; but by treating the dry tropical heat like that of an Italian summer, even with my easily-tanned skin I got myself a third degree burn right across my chest. It called for instant medical attention and taught me a most painful and unsightly lesson. After a fortnight in Montego Bay we drove up the coast to Ocho Rios, and the recently-built Sans Souci Hotel. Apart from the main building at the top of a steep hill and, at the bottom, a swimming-pool a few feet above sea level, the place looked as if it had been 'planned' by throwing a handful of bungalows with verandahs against the slope and letting them stick where they'd landed. Paths wound round them and, at night, large pop-eyed toads would straddle the gravel croaking their love-songs in the brilliant moonlight.

Although Greville and I had forgotten the world, Jean and her lawyers were still well and truly on the warpath. They got on to some local but decidedly amateur sleuths. Their attempts to catch us *in flagrante delicto* were hilariously infantile and not very easy for them because we always had our own rooms under our own names. Wherever Greville and I went, pairs of shiny black eyes would peer out from the bushes, and large figures would loom up behind doors, then dive into the darkness. After the initial shock Greville and I roared with laughter each time and would jump out at them saying 'Boo', at which they'd yelp as if they'd been hit and scuttle into the shrubbery.

I must mention Kay Bieber at this point. Kay, an attractive blonde, was Sans Souci's 'hostess'. She took enormous trouble to make all the guests happy and endeared herself to us immediately. It was with Kay that I trekked up into the hills behind Ocho Rios. We'd been told about an amazing witch-doctor-cum-clairvoyant, and we routed him out of his lair one afternoon. Kay and I still remember very clearly his words that day:

'You are married now, but you love someone else,' he said, and went on, 'you will eventually marry this other man and will be very happy with him. But he will die suddenly and when he is still young.'

I walked down that hill in a desperate daze and Kay told me only recently that I was sobbing my heart out. Over the years that prediction was to haunt me.

Another amazing thing happened to us in Ocho Rios, and it certainly made us realize what is meant by 'American hospitality'.

We were having a drink one evening in the bar of Sans Souci when Kay came over with a handsome couple. Probably in their forties, both tall, dark and dressed with casual chic, they made a striking pair.

'I'd like you to meet Carl and Louise Friedlander,' she said. 'They've just got in from New York and are staying here a couple of weeks before going on to Montego Bay.' Chairs were pulled up, glasses filled and we all chatted away happily. Now, this was at a time when the British weren't allowed to spend any foreign currency, particularly dollars, and although Greville and I would have loved to visit the States it was definitely out of bounds. But we asked a lot of questions about America and said we hoped we would be able to go over there another year. Then the Friedlanders told us about their flat in New York; their interest in painting and the theatre; and their plans to come over to Britain for a visit in the near future. We decided we all liked each other enormously and with a 'see you by the pool in the morning' went our separate ways.

The next day, however, friends of the Friedlanders turned up unexpectedly in Montego Bay and they switched plans to join them and instead of meeting us by the pool, Kay handed us a chunky envelope. I opened it, and two keys on a ring fell out, plus a wad of US dollars in a rubber band. The letter-heading bore a number on Park Avenue, New York. I read the words out loud: 'So sorry we may not see you again this time, but here are the keys to our apartment in New York. We've already wired our maid, who will expect you if you let her know which day you will arrive. Please use everything. Our clothes should more or less fit you, and Louise's furs will probably be useful for Kate in New York's bitter winter. Make yourselves at home, and we look forward to seeing you again either in England or America another year.'

Kay, Greville and I handed the letter from one to another. We each read it again in stunned silence; we couldn't believe it. Even in those far-off days when one left cars unlocked and trusted people in general, this seemed like a fairy-tale. We pinched ourselves all the way to New York, but it wasn't a dream. The apartment was there, and so was the maid with a broad built-in grin on her shiny black face. There were flowers in all the rooms, champagne on ice, and the wardrobes full of the most gorgeous his and her clothes. And the bed – oh! the size of it – a real playground, and the ceiling above was one huge looking-glass with stars and a half crescent moon which could light up in the dark. How grateful we were to Carl and Louise for their hospitality. We stayed one unforgettable week in New York.

We learnt such a lot about each other on that first holiday, and how wonderful it was to find the same things mattered to both of us. Not only did we share a sense of fun and sense of humour, but also a respect and caring for other people. I mention this and it might sound a trivial detail to many, but the importance that both Greville and I gave to good manners played an extremely important part in our life together. Greville had an inborn kindness and instinctive consideration, which was quite remarkable, for people in general, and for me in particular, and nobody appreciated it more than I did.

Back in London we found we still had to play the waiting game. But when you know where you want to go in life and have an ever-deepening relationship with the one person you want and who wants to go with you, it doesn't really matter if you find a few obstacles on the way. I was also very happy in my work.

In Edinburgh's Usher Hall we were showing Norman Hartnell's first 'ready-to-wear' collection. Yes, it was the great Sir Norman who blazed the trail for top designers into the 'off-the-peg' fields. Norman Hartnell was always imaginative and I can still see him standing elegantly on the bare stage and hear him say to the producer, Michael Whittaker, 'This silver city in the land of heather calls for the softest grey and lilac finale.' And minions were promptly dispatched to collect mammoth bouquets of mauve heather. This was just as well, because by some horrible error, what were expected to be beautifully-fitting grey evening dresses turned out to be outsize tents. So, as we sailed up for that final scene and dipped low into our royal curtsies (Norman attracted royalty like a magnet!), we were each clutching yards of superfluous material to our bellies behind strategically-placed bouquets of heather. There always seemed to be fun and friendliness working with Normie and Michael.

Greville also introduced me to another world: that of horse-racing. Flat-racing in particular had always been Greville's great love – although soccer and cricket ran a dead heat for second place after his double blue days at Cambridge.

The race course is very much a club and both Jean and Greville were long-time members. As in most clubs, gossip runs rife. Everyone not only knew, but seemed to be inordinately interested in the fact that Jean and Greville were splitting up; so when I appeared in the Members' Enclosure with him, heads turned, tongues wagged and I felt decidedly uncomfortable. Although the whole thing was absurdly petty, neither of us was thick-skinned, so we appreciated in full those racing stalwarts who knew both Greville and Jean, but snorted at such behaviour and showed us friendship over the years. Amongst the many people who did so were the late Lord (Harry) Rosebery and his still formidable wife, Eva; Lady Rosebery's enchantingly kind daughter Lavinia, Duchess of Norfolk; the late Lord Belper; old Porchey (the present Earl of Carnarvon); Monica Sheriffe, the owner of that lovely horse 'Never Say Die'; the trainer of the 1974 Derby winner 'Snow Knight', Peter Nelson and his Irish wife, Mackie; Lord and Lady Willoughby de Broke; Tigie and Tom Nicholls, who wrote for the *Sporting Chronicle*; and that other veteran journalist Quinny Gilbey; ITV commentator Tony Cooke and his gravel-voiced wife Peta; and the one and only Peter O'Sullevan.

I also warmed to certain book-makers on the rails, and they certainly didn't grin at us because we lost our boots to them. I've hardly ever made a bet in my life and Greville was one of that rare breed of permanently-successful backers over many years. He was a lucky owner too. He had winners with John Dunlop and Ted Smythe, but there was a special magic in his partnership with the late Stafford Ingham. 'Staff' at that time was becoming a brilliant trainer of two-year-olds, and with Greville owning and him training, it sometimes seemed that even a three-legged horse would win for them. In the very early days there was 'Sally Rose', the lovely grey filly 'Susannah', 'Light Catch' and the great character 'Plymouth Fair', who raced on for many years. He loved marshmallows and knew exactly how important it was that he should win.

Then came the excitement of owning 'Richer', cleverly named

because he was by 'Rockefella' out of 'Granpa's Will': it was early in February 1952 that Staff asked Greville, 'Do you want glory or cash? or shall we go out for both and win the Cambridgeshire?' The months that followed had all the ups and downs, inflated hopes and let-down luck of a Nat Gould story. But it ended on a brilliantly-sunny October day when Ken Gethin and 'Richer' flew in first past the post at Newmarket and did indeed win the Cambridgeshire. It was a brilliant training feat and the thrill was tremendous.

I'll never forget the joy when 'Caterina', the filly Greville named after me, won at Goodwood and then, a few weeks later, the Fresh-water Stakes Cup at Ascot. How I cried, despite the price, to see her go under the auctioneer's hammer not so many months later. It's no good pretending that I enjoyed regular everyday racing. I'm quite sure that if we'd had a small stud (Greville's unfulfilled dream) it would have been different. As it was, I knew that every horse Greville bought would, relatively soon, have to be sold, and every time this broke my heart. I couldn't bear to think where they'd go to next and what their end would be.

Greville never quite believed me, but I was perfectly content to drive him to and from the racecourses, then spend the afternoon comfortably writing or reading in the car. At the beginning I really did try to share Greville's interest. I even bought a small note-book in which, at the start of every flat-racing season, I wrote all the two-year-olds to 'watch', their breeding, their owners and their colours; but whereas I usually absorb information quite quickly, all this just would not sink in. At one point I also decided to listen when going round stables and learn some racing jargon. Phrases like: 'he stands over a lot of ground', 'what a genuine head', 'built to stay', 'an early sprinter', 'good bone' etc. etc. But after dubbing the Queen's brilliant filly, 'Aureole', a 'Rabbity little thing', I decided not to put my 'knowledge' into practice again.

Greville even bought me a horse called 'Fast and Friendly'. He proved to be both, and the first day he won I flung my arms enthu-siastically around Jeremy Tree. 'Wasn't that wonderful,' I cried. 'He won, he won!' Jeremy smiled rather wanly – his horse had come in second! Incidentally it was my 'Fast and Friendly' who inspired

Peter O'Sullevan to call his next horse 'Just Friendly', and it was the first in a marvellous string of well-deserved successes for Peter.

No, I just didn't have the right mentality for racing. Of course I loved it when Greville had a winner, but when someone congratulated me for winning a race I felt I was flying under false colours – I hadn't chosen the horse, ridden, trained or paid for it (Greville footed all those bills), so why should I be congratulated for everyone else's efforts? Silly, maybe, but there it is: the Sport of Kings and I were decidedly incompatible.

Greville and I, however, were becoming increasingly compatible, and we provided lots of fodder for racecourse gossip. Even without Richard's help, and despite the fact that it was she who walked out on Greville, Jean slapped in a divorce petition citing me. Greville persuaded me to object on principle so, in a blaze of front-page publicity, I was dismissed from the case and we were back to square one. Not that this mattered much, because there was still a while before Richard's three-year plan could be set in motion. But a sign of those times hit me hard. One just didn't get cited in divorce suits with impunity – certainly not in the eyes of the BBC. It wasn't long before Cecil McGivern summoned me solemnly to his office at Lime Grove.

Cecil was a strange, tied-up-in-knots sort of man. A Catholic, he drank willingly, chain-smoked (unfortunately in bed too, as he died dramatically one night when his sheets caught fire), and he hid behind thick horn-rimmed glasses, a fleeting smile and nervous movements. Although I quite liked him, I never felt he fitted comfortably into his role of TV programme controller. That morning he hummed and hawed a bit, but his message was simple: I was going to be dropped from 'Quite Contrary' and he was 'sorry, but ...' I couldn't appear on the BBC while my private life was so 'muddled'. As ITV was not yet born, that meant I was wiped clean off the television screen.

I was not only shocked by this news, but also extremely worried because television, my first excursions into radio and the personal appearances which were the direct consequence of both mediums were my only source of income (not very great anyway with Mr Winnick taking his 50%). Greville was, as ever, a tower of strength. He understood that I didn't want him to 'keep' me, but his generosity and the thoughtfulness of his presents over the depressing months to follow was overwhelming: hampers of food, interesting little parcels with bath oil, soap and stockings would arrive in the nick of time.

Luckily, the press were more lenient towards my behaviour than the BBC. It was the *Sunday Graphic* who first asked me to write a weekly column for them on Fashion and Beauty. My dislike of having someone else do a job which I might get credit for made things slightly difficult. What sounds so easy – 500-odd words on a subject one enjoys - is, in fact, extremely difficult for someone with neither training nor previous experience. I produced my copy on time but it must have rated the worst on record – what came out in the paper was virtually a re-write. It simply meant that just as I'd done on television – sailing on with not the slightest idea what I was doing, or even how to do it – I was now doing in journalism. Once again I could only hope to learn, right out there in front of the public.

Don't let anyone tell me that all journalists are a bunch of hard-drinking, cynical toughies. It would take up a whole page to list the names of those who have encouraged me and generously given me sound practical advice since those early days. And I must say that, in retrospect, I find it very interesting to note that there is a great solidarity amongst the female of the species. I listened gratefully and learnt a lot from such fashion queens as Iris Ashley, Ernestine Carter, Winifride Jackson and that enchanting all-rounder Felicity Green; the lovely Joyce Hopkirk, who was my direct and brilliant boss as Woman's Editor on the *Sun*, the doyenne with infinite wisdom Marge Proops, and I could never leave out the supposed 'Arch Bitch' of Fleet Street, who has a heart even greater than her magnificent presence – Jean Rook (and I bet she'll kill me for saying so).

However slowly you feel it is dragging, time does always pass. Greville eventually got his divorce by what was laughingly called 'giving evidence' – i.e. spending an innocent night with a willing stranger at a London hotel and making sure at least one member of the staff saw them both in an intimate state of disarray the next morning. And Richard eventually filed his suit for desertion against me.

The actual day of the case, in spring 1955, affected us both deeply.

I stayed indoors and alone until Richard telephoned me as soon as he had left the court. Even though I knew that this was what I had wanted, a desperate sadness and a deep sense of failure enveloped me. I put the telephone down and it rang again almost immediately. I picked it up to hear Gilbert Harding's voice. He was asking me to join him on some personal appearance, but his friendly gruffness released my pent-up tears, and all I could do was sob down the line, 'I've just been divorced, Gilbert, I've just been divorced.' 'Oh, my poor darling,' he sympathized, then there was a click and he was gone.

It couldn't have been more than half an hour later that the doorbell rang, and a small messenger stood there submerged by a mammoth mass of flowers. The card read: 'Katie. My fond love and understanding – Gilbert' and was written in his own hand. This was a typically warm, personal gesture from that great character and meant a lot to me on that bitter-sweet day.

How often I have wished my emotions didn't run so deep. On the other hand, being torn apart by one's feelings is counterbalanced by an ability to enjoy happiness in all its subtleties and to the full. And when that divorce day ended with Richard coming round to have a drink with Greville and myself, I remember looking from one to the other. I felt desperately selfish to be happy and free to marry Greville at the expense of hurting Richard; the fact that he was behaving with such understanding made it so much worse.

A New
World

At the end of that summer in 1955, nearly four years after we fell in love, Greville and I were married. I would never have believed that a flimsy legal document could add a new dimension to a relationship we both already felt was near-perfect. The ceremony was simple, the surroundings stark, nothing really warmed up the bareness of the Registry Office. We chose Chelsea because it was near Cranmer Court where I had a small flat. Photographers framed our path. We dived off to the airport and onto a plane for Naples – but not before Greville had rung up for the result for the 2.30 race! He'd won – we felt it was a good omen!

That evening we had a delicious fish dinner at a small restaurant at the harbourside, and spent a romantic night in an hotel high on the hill overlooking the fairy-lit bay of Naples. The next morning saw us off across the bay to Ischia. We spent most of the following fortnight in the sea because, for some unknown reason, the water supply on the whole island was cut off.

On our return journey we stopped off in Rome, and I took Greville to the Sacred Heart. I wanted to introduce him to some of my special teachers. The first person we ran into was Mother Sanga. I flung myself into her arms: 'This is my husband. I know you'll approve of him, he's wonderful,' I burbled. They shook hands, and then she turned to me quizzically. Suddenly I remembered; about seven years before, I'd brought Richard, my first husband, to the Sacred Heart soon after we'd got married. I must have blanched with embarrassment, but she held me tight, then stepped back and put her hands together and, looking at me as though I were a naughty child, said, '*Adesso basta, Caterinella, adesso basta*' – 'Now that's enough, Caterinella, that's enough'.

From Rome we flew straight back to England and settled into a marriage which was destined to have many highs and a few lows, but was never lacking in love and was never dull.

Apart from being a married woman again, I was now also a step-mother. Mark, Greville's son by his first wife, was eleven years old. Of course I'd seen a great deal of him during the previous four years and, even though I'd never had much to do with children, was very fond of him. But neither Greville nor I were patient people, and although he was tremendously protective towards his son and loved him dearly, it was a bitter disappointment that Mark hadn't inherited any of his love of sports. What's more Mark's mother, who lived in Jamaica, apart from being the worst letter-writer in the world, showed a singular lack of interest in him. This upset Mark greatly; he had an adoration for his out-of-sight parent, so there were many times that I pretended a letter had arrived from her, and then read a scribbled rigmarole of my own, full of imaginative details of a life I knew nothing about.

Despite an undoubtedly erratic childhood, Mark is now a surprisingly well-adjusted individual; he is happily married with two children, Samantha and Catherine – yes, Kate is called after me, and I regard this with pride as an unexpected seal of approval on what I've always felt was my inadequate, though very willing, stepmotherhood.

Once my private life was tidied up again the BBC welcomed me back into the fold, but just about the same time, Independent Television was born and Associated Rediffusion signed me up on an exclusive two-year contract. Advertising magazines (ad mags) were the rage then – one or two presenters sauntered slowly round a well-laden set, and took it in turns to extol the virtues of various products.

Alan (Fluff) Freeman had recently arrived from Australia, and made his first TV appearances on one of these series. He was always great fun to work with, even before he found his very successful DJ niche, and he swears I once stopped him from taking refuge in a wardrobe when he forgot his lines. Of course, there were few aids such as autocues then.

Apart from my regular television shows, I was hopping around like an agitated flea on a great number of other commitments. I found it very galling to be slogging like a Trojan and, at the same time, have people come up to me and say, 'Oh, I haven't seen you on the television lately – stopped working, have you?' It's infuriating that people automatically assume you're totally inactive if you don't appear on television. I've always felt that, when I've not been tethered to a regular weekly show, I've worked hardest – either alone at my desk writing or on whistle-stop jobs in Britain or abroad. There are so many spin-offs from appearing on television, including opening all kinds of shops, addressing meetings and introducing fashion shows galore – and Reid & Taylor Spectaculars.

Reid & Taylor is a relatively small firm in Scotland which produces the 'most expensive twist worsted in the world' and has at its helm John Packer. John started with Reid & Taylor as the original whizz-kid. He is a small, good-looking and flamboyantly-dressed man with big ideas which have turned the firm into one of Britain's most successful exporters. The firm's 'spectaculars' started when John enlisted the aid of Norman Hartnell, myself, some beautiful male models and a Boeing 707. The plane took us on the first promotional tour, covering five European countries in two days. My role was to present the shows in the various languages.

Each time we landed we had speedy scene-shifts because the seats had to be moved from their normal front-facing position and placed around the edge of the plane, thus leaving the centre free as a catwalk. It was an extraordinary experience, made even more exhausting for me because I had a dreadful cold that blocked my head and I could only get some slight relief by lying upside-down with my feet above my head every time we took off.

This trip in the Boeing 707 was only one of John Packer's promotions that I took part in; amongst others were his 'take-overs' of Gleneagles in Scotland and Nostell Priory, where all the local hearses for miles around were commandeered to collect an enormous number of European VIPs from the station and take them, at a funereal pace, up the winding drive to the priory. Then there was the year we went deep into the Moet & Chandon champagne caves in Epernay, another time to the beautiful palace of Ca' Pesaro on the Grand Canal in Venice, and most recently to Leeds Castle, which looked glorious floodlit under a full moon. The spectaculars were all very hard work, but tremendously exhilarating and well-organized.

On several of these tours I've had the pleasure of being presented to Princess Margaret and I've noticed so often how unflagging and cheerfully conscientious she is.

I often wonder how this dignified, even nose-in-the-air, image has built up around me. Everyone seems to have forgotten the crazy antics I got up to with the Goons on television. They were all together then – Spike Milligan, Harry Secombe, Peter Sellers and Michael Bentine, beautifully supported by Kenneth Connor and Graham Stark. Amongst many other indignities they submitted me to, they had me dressed in woolly long-johns, blown up when riding an elephant, shot out of a cannon and submerged under buckets of water. After one such dowsing, Michael Bentine and I hadn't time to really dry off before the studios shut down for the night, so he and I turned up as two decidedly damp rats at Birmingham's eminently respectable Grand Hotel. We were faced by great disapproval and it was only after lengthy persuasion that the night porter would give us our keys.

My first encounter, many years ago, with one particular Goon (when both he and I had yet to become familiar faces) was, to say the least, traumatic. I was driving from Hyde Park towards Lowndes Square (one way streets were rare around London in those days). The lights were green as I crossed Knightsbridge, but halfway across I saw a mammoth car racing towards me. I pressed down on the accelerator, but not quite fast enough – the giant limousine caught my rear door at full-pelt. With a screech of brakes, a crunch of steel and not a second to think, I was spun round to face the park exit again! I was stunned for a second; then my first thought was for my small dog. She'd been flung off the ledge behind the back seat, but luckily looked more indignant than injured.

I grabbed her to me and we shot out of the car to face a splutteringly apologetic man. The more he apologized, the louder I shouted in fear and anger. From the height of my Latin rage I suddenly noticed we were ringed by policemen. They had been escorting Harry Secombe to a police ball. Harry confirmed his apologies the next day with a magnificent bouquet. Funny to think a few seconds difference and it could so easily have been a wreath. As it was, he endeared himself firmly to me forever.

In a general air of lunacy, all the Goons worked like beavers to make the end results appear effortless, but certain streaks of craziness overlapped into their private lives. Take Peter Sellers for instance. He's always been mad about cars, and at that time his great love was a brand new, pale silver-blue Jaguar. This treasure developed a small but persistent knocking for which no clues could be found under the dashboard or bonnet. It was his loyal, long-suffering friend Graham Stark who offered to be shut inside the boot to find out if that was nearer the source of the noise.

Very soon Peter, forgetting about poor Graham, stopped at a pub for a drink, then got back into the car and drove off with his chum still in the boot. Brought down to earth by a loud thumping at the back of the car, he leapt out only to find the boot was firmly jammed. In a panic, Peter drove around looking for a garage to help him. With none in sight, he stopped to have another go himself. This time, after an extra strong tug, the catch gave way and out staggered Graham. The fumes had doped him badly. A woman passing by, quite certain she was witness to a kidnapping, started to scream. Then, recognizing the two men, she hurled insults at Peter, took his car number and rushed off, vowing to tell the police and the world in general about 'the wicked Mr Sellers'. With Graham by now fully conscious, this tirade of abuse banished their fears and triggered off helpless laughter between these two great chums.

Dick Lester directed the Goon series; and brilliant Dick, who has gone on to further and greater fame on the larger screen via the first Beatles film, Rita Tushingham's *The Knack*, *The Three Musketeers* etc., had an endearing and most effective 'switch off' technique. In the face of many a temperamental eruption amongst this group of genius comedians, he'd face the wall, tilt backwards in a hard chair, and play his clarinet with his eyes closed, until the atmosphere had sweetened again.

As well as the Goons, I loved being involved with Arthur Askey and Bud Flanagan of the Crazy Gang. We were invited to appear in a sketch together in the 1954 Royal Variety Performance. As it was the 25th anniversary of this show, I had the chance of meeting other wonderful artists such as Arthur Askey, Jack Buchanan, Gladys Cooper, Noël Coward, Michael Denison, Dulcie Gray, Leslie Henson, Ted Heath, Bob Hope, Jack Hylton, Frankie Howerd, Howard Keel, Nigel Patrick, Elsie Randolph, Al Read, Peter Sellers, Dickie Valentine, Norman Wisdom and Donald Wolfit.

For my role I had the excitement of being dressed by the late Victor Stiebel. He made a splendid dress for me; it had a flowing black velvet skirt, and the 'off one shoulder' crimson velvet bodice gripped me tightly round the ribs. The overall effect was of glamorous dignity, so the incongruity was complete when, to the lively strains of ' "*Boyled" Beef & Carrots*', I traipsed down an aisle, on to the impressive Palladium stage to play Bud Flannagan's mother-in-law.

My father's reaction to my divorce was unexpectedly mild. 'I knew that nice boy Richard would be no match for Caterinella in the long run,' was all he said. He was also surprisingly curious to meet Greville. I had tried to give Greville an accurate outline of my background – not an easy task because he was basically very conventional and, I felt, dismissed my accounts of my younger life as somewhat exaggerated ... until we flew over to Switzerland together for a family reunion.

My heart was beating hard and I was full of trepidation as we landed at Cointrin, Geneva's Airport. How would these two strong personalities react to each other? My father was waiting for us just beyond the barrier. He was a large man, but his bulky fur-lined overcoat, with its wide Astrakhan collar, made me think that he'd put on a lot of weight since we last met, and his matching black Astrakhan Russian-style hat accentuated his Slav features and pale blue eyes.

My half-sister Margherita, and half-brother Enrico, about ten and eight years old by now, clung on to his hands on either side. A few steps away stood Mademoiselle Anne Marie Tache, their governess and my father's friend, who had accompanied them all to London a few years before.

Clashing emotions always ran very deep and strong between my father and myself, but today Love surfaced, and as I felt his arms fold round me in an emotional bear hug, I knew we were both crying again. Then, unlocking himself from me he placed both arms round Greville, embraced him warmly and kissed him firmly on both cheeks. 'Welcome my son, welcome!' he said with tears flowing through a beaming smile. Greville, having expected a handshake, looked visibly shaken, but my father's warmth overwhelmed him and I noticed that Greville's eyes were glistening too.

Then, when we were all bundled into the car, Papa began: 'Caterinella told me you like oysters and champagne, so I've booked a table where they specialize in that kind of lunch.'

The tone was set, and we were ushered to a large table near a window. Within minutes my father had told Greville how much he was going to love him, had offered him a well-stacked money-clip made out of a heavy gold Mexican coin, and was pouring out all our family problems: 'I will show you the documentation when we get home.' True to his word, Papa later brought out what he called his 'duplicates' and 'triplicates', which we pored over until we were cross-eyed, especially Greville, whose Italian and French were in the 'left over from schooldays' class. But we did gather that a number of litigations were underway and that Augusta, his third wife and mother of Enrico and Margherita, was fighting a winning battle (quite rightly, but much to my father's disgust) against his efforts to put her into a mental establishment similar to the one in which he'd kept me.

That weekend was the first time I'd felt close to my father since I was a very small child. Suddenly, all the bitterness between us had vanished. I'm quite sure Greville was the catalyst because by being married to him I felt protected and, therefore, relaxed; whilst Papa, in turn, knew he'd met his match in Greville and could intimidate me no longer. All the same, on the Monday, we were exhausted, emotionally drained and absolutely delighted to be flying back to London.

There was a letter waiting for me from the BBC, and Tom Sloan, at that time Assistant Head of Light Entertainment, suggested I should go and see him to 'talk things over', as he put it.

Tom's office was tucked in at the back of the TV Centre, which was still being built. It was a pokey set-up and decidedly a halfway house to his impressive and permanent fourth-floor realm. That morning I certainly didn't realize just how important and far-reaching the effects of this first meeting were to prove. I immediately took to Queenie Lipyeat, Tom's secretary, who was always to be his valuable right hand. Attractive, red-haired and very reassuring, she seemed to sense my non-stop chatter was a cover-up for a very bad attack of nerves! Dear 'Queen Bee', as I dubbed her, was destined to become a very close friend.

Tom and I had a long talk. We thrashed over the subject of television in general and he asked me how, or rather if, I saw my own role developing. I liked this solidly-built man with his round face, bristling moustache, twinkling eyes and quick sense of humour. As I left his office he shook my hand warmly saying, 'You really are an intelligent girl, aren't you? Completely different from the one who appears on the small screen!' I roared with laughter, and that was the beginning of an important friendship which lasted until Tom died when he was in his early fifties.

That first meeting with Tom was destined to change my career, but not straight away. In the meantime it was the start of his lasting friendship with Greville and myself, and the start of his role as adviser in my life. I ran to him with every professional problem and soon discovered that I could take his advice with confidence. It was Tom who introduced me to the man who has been my agent (without a contract) for many a long year – Bunny Lewis. Bunny was just right. A strange, complex, contradictory character with a big heart he often tries to hide. He never speaks of the Military Cross he won in Italy, nor of being mentioned in despatches; but he is proud of his long spell as Decca's Head of Promotion, of being chosen Top European as well as Top British Record Producer, and of his award-winning songs: Edith Piaf's 'Milord', 'Cara Mia' and 'No Greater Love' amongst them. Bunny and his very attractive French wife, Janique, became our fast and lasting friends.

Holidays played a big part in my life with Greville. Luckily, ours was a volatile marriage with frequent eruptions which, no doubt whatever, were valuable safety valves for us both. There were no sulks on either side and Greville had the incredible ability to say he was sorry, even when he was in the right. But the stresses and strains of everyday living, his racing and the endless variety of my activities were great. They could so easily have sneaked a destructive wedge between us, so I'm quite sure those breaks we had together were the welders and sometimes the re-welders of our relationship.

We always chose late January to early March to escape to the sun. It was a blissful 'do nothing much' existence with lots of sunbathing, swimming, walking, reading and early nights; but above all, we had the time to talk, to catch up any threads that might have become tangled during the past year.

We worked the whole year with those happy holidays in mind and had a holiday pig which grew fat on the inflated prices we charged ourselves for not going to restaurants and night-clubs – no sacrifice this, as we enjoyed nothing more than staying at home together. Looking back, I'm quite sure all those years of regular, peaceful holidays together contributed not only to our relationship but also to our enduring good health.

It was in Tobago that a very special friendship was born – between Clive and Millie Brook and us. It started one evening at the Bacolet Inn where all of us were staying. Greville and I were having a late-night stroll before going to bed when a small, very pretty woman with large blue eyes and dark wavy hair darted out from the bushes. She spoke softly and quickly, and looked rather like a naughty child playing truant and afraid of being caught.

'I believe you and my husband are in the same line of business – his name is Clive Brook, I'm afraid he's not very sociable, but I do hope we'll see you, on the beach perhaps?' With that she was gone. Greville and I looked at each other in silence. Clive Brook. To my eternally film-struck mind, the name conjured up all the glamour of Hollywood stardom: *Cavalcade*, *Shanghai Express*, *The Four Feathers* and many other films. I must admit the face was a bit of a blur to my memory, but I knew it was a very handsome one.

'Oh! Greville. Clive Brook. How exciting!' I cooed with delight.

Next morning he was my first thought. And there was a solitary swimmer in the Bacolet Bay as we walked down to the beach. 'That's Clive Brook,' I exclaimed, and before Greville could stop me, I'd dived into the water in pursuit. I soon caught up with my prey. 'Good morning,' I smiled brightly.

'It certainly is.' His smile was not encouraging, but I carried on.

'Do you swim a long way every morning?'

'Usually.' This time he turned slightly and began swimming a little faster – away from me. But it wasn't difficult to keep up.

'Staying long are you?' then not waiting for a reply, 'I've always admired you so much!'

No sound, so I went on: 'You were so marvellous in *Gioconda Smile*.' Still no reply, and it was taking a little more effort for me to keep up with the film-star now. But I persevered, even though he wasn't saying much.

It was a small bay and when we got to the furthest point, I realized he was going to swim round it. Anyway, Greville was beckoning to me from the shore by now, so after a cheerful 'Goodbye, I'll see you soon!' I swam back.

'Oh, darling, he's wonderful!' I cried rushing out of the water.

'Who?' asked Greville.

'Why, Clive Brook of course. I've just swum all across the bay with him.'

'You're very clever,' came his quiet reply, 'because Clive Brook has been sitting under that palm tree for ages reading the *Financial Times*, and I've been talking shares with him for the past half-hour.'

During one of our holidays in Grenada, I was summoned back to London by the BBC. It was to introduce the Ivor Novello Awards and I was thrilled to be asked. Unfortunately it hardly turned out as I'd hoped.

The flight back was badly delayed, and I was knocked out by an exaggerated attack of jet-lag. What's more, we arrived so late that I had to dive off the plane straight into rehearsals. The programme was going out, live of course, from Shepherd's Bush Theatre and was getting lots of publicity. I came in for a good deal of that too, so the adrenalin was flowing despite my exhaustion.

The time drew near and we all gathered backstage. There was Cliff Richard, Matt Munro, Billy Butlin, who was presenting the Awards, songwriter Paddy Roberts, and many more besides. As I paced up and down, Helen Shapiro said, 'I don't know what you're worried about, you only have to talk.' Then the orchestra struck up and it was countdown.

As I walked onto that stage, my mind went blank. I couldn't have told you where I was or what I was doing. The music stopped, the applause died down, I opened my mouth to say what? – I didn't know – no matter because nothing came out!

How long could this have lasted? I felt it went on for ever, this total, horrible 'dry', and I didn't even have the presence of mind to admit to it and ask for help. All I could think of was that I'd been flown halfway across the world to behave like this. How shaming! At last someone prompted me from under the camera. Thank God he'd pressed my starter, and away I went. But that evening sticks out embarrassingly as one of my worst professional experiences.

During another holiday in Tobago, in February 1962, a telegram arrived to say that my father had died in the Nestlé Hospital, Lausanne. Although the news wasn't unexpected – he'd had a number of strokes – I was knocked for six. This character who had inspired so much love, fear and even hate in me at times had seemed immortal.

My flashbacks of our relationship were so vivid, so mangling. A few months before, Greville and I had flown over to see him again. Despite three strokes, he was still in fighting form and was talking Russian to his sister, French to the children, Italian to his wife, Augusta, who had rejoined him, and English to Greville and me. And only Greville, by threatening to call the police if he didn't stop bullying everyone, managed to get some order into that crazy household. But now he was dead and I couldn't stop sobbing my heart out.

I wanted to fly to Switzerland at once, but the funeral was the following day, so Greville persuaded me to be sensible. All the same I was determined to telephone my step-mother. Maybe it's easier nowadays, but then it was difficult enough to ring Trinidad from Tobago, let alone Europe. 'I want to speak to the Marquise Imperiali,' I kept repeating to puzzled operators. I tried and tried again. Eventually a bright girl in Trinidad got the message, and obviously realizing I was het up, she said very soothingly, 'Yes, yes, don't worry. I know, you want to speak to the Monkeys in Lausanne!'

Out of
Step

About this time, in the early sixties, there seemed to be a handful of years when everything happened at a helter-skelter rate. 1961 was the first year that I introduced the Eurovision Song Contest. This first programme played a big part in accelerating my career but as it was such an important milestone and my connection with the show spanned fourteen years, I'd like to concentrate on it later.

It was about this time too that, from a holiday in Barbados, we rushed to New York where I'd been booked to appear as a guest panellist on the American counterparts of 'What's My Line?' and 'I've Got A Secret' as well as other TV shows. It was there that I met Margaret Truman, a warm sweet person who was still concentrating on her singing career. Her agent/manager fixed a screen test for me, and suddenly I was in the running as Lana Turner's sister. This was something I'd always dreamed about – me in a Hollywood movie!

The time for Greville to go back to England had come, so I waved him goodbye and then scurried around New York buying far too many clothes for my big moment, with no time to think about anything else. The great day dawned and I was off to the airport. The flight from New York to Los Angeles was up on the board. At that moment, I heard another one called from New York to London. An awful emptiness grabbed my guts. What on earth was I doing? Flying even further away from Greville. Suddenly there was no real excitement without him, and I realized that my name in lights would never be any substitute for our happy marriage. Never have I moved so fast. I cancelled my ticket to L.A. and in less than half an hour all my new clothes and I were flying back to London and Greville.

I'm well aware that my greatest shortcoming is to act first and think later, but this is one occasion that I've never had cause to regret my impulsive nature. Even if I'd had the slightest doubt, the enthusiastic, surprised joy with which Greville welcomed me back, and the happiness I felt in seeing him again, would have swept it away.

Back in England the work rolled in. Tom Sloan came up with the idea of 'Golden Girl', a TV soap-opera-cum-thriller, all about 'the richest girl in the world', with each episode ending in true cliffhanger style. It ran for two summers. Apart from me, the cast was made up of real and enduring actors like Faith Brook, Patrick Barr, David Langton, Wilfrid Brambell, Moira Redmond, Francis Matthews, Edward Judd and many more besides.

I enjoyed 'acting' and so I leapt at the offer of making a film in Italy. I remember being terribly hurt though when I discovered they were going to dub my voice. Surely I spoke my father tongue well enough not to warrant that! I don't know whether I was more relieved or ashamed when I found the real reason for the dubbing was my lack of acting talent.

Undeterred, I next accepted to play Richard Todd's wife in a forgettable film called *Intent to Kill* (it is still shown at regular if only occasional intervals on TV, so you can probably see what I mean). Most of the critics ignored my performance, but one did compare my rage in a matrimonial fight with Richard to the hissing of an empty, left-on kettle!

Bloodied, but still unbowed, I let myself be persuaded to appear with Evelyn Laye and Marie Löhr as Frank Lawton's mistress in a play called *Silver Wedding*. I'm very glad I did the play because, apart from anything else, it brought me their valuable friendship, and, most rewarding of all, that of the director Charles Hickman. Ever since he has remained a pillar of wisdom, kindness and humour in my life.

The play was on tour when my name came up. For some reason Joan Benham couldn't come into London with it and I was picked to replace her. When you think of that clever actress, it was a foolhardy task for me to take on. I can't remember much about that performance, but I do know I had an excellent exit line. I had to turn at the door and ask my lover's wife, Evelyn Laye, 'has anyone ever told you you're a bitch?'

Any actress worthy of her name could have got a round of applause on that line at every performance. Me? Well I played in *Silver Wedding* for over six months in London and occasionally, by accident, I did get a faint ripple.

But then, one night six years later I was having dinner with Charles, and suddenly, 'I know exactly how to say that line!' I cried. 'Listen!' and said it.

'You're quite right, Kate, that is absolutely perfect! What a pity it's just a little late.'

As a little light relief from my Thespian activities I decided to become a business woman. Well, it didn't quite start out like that. What actually happened was that my agent booked me to compère a fashion show in Llandudno for a Mr and Mrs Eastwood. Now, somewhere along the way, and nothing whatsoever to do with the Eastwoods, I'd picked up the information that to invest in the Coin-Operated Dry-Cleaning boom was *the* way to make a fortune. Since hard work had done nothing for me on that score it sounded like an excellent idea.

As I was bidding a cordial goodbye to Bill and Dorothy Eastwood after a most successful fashion show, this must have been to the forefront of my mind. So much so that, to my amazement, I heard myself asking my new-found friends of twenty-four hours standing, 'How do you feel about coming in as partners with me in a Coin-Op Dry-Cleaning venture?' As the subject hadn't even been mentioned before, they looked understandably surprised. But I chatted on merrily, now convincing myself, and perhaps just a little them, that Coin-Op Dry-Cleaning was the best thing since wholemeal toast.

When I got back to London I said to Greville, 'Darling, I think I may have gone into the dry-cleaning business.'

'Oh dear!' was his only comment.

A few months later, in a brand-new shopping precinct in the small town of Bromborough, Cheshire, hidden well away from all passing trade, and backing on to a bomb-site sparsely used as a car park, our little shop appeared. Smartly-pillared, painted green and white, and with my fascimile signature blazened across the front door, it looked wonderful. Financially, however, it was a total disaster. Complicated machinery, bad servicing, staff problems, floods and fires all added to our problems. Above all, most of the time neither Bill, Dorothy nor I could be around to 'mind our own business' as it were.

I know. Who in their right mind would launch a shop in Cheshire while working from London, especially as Bill and Dorothy, living in Hightown, already had a successful engineering business plus their fashion sideline in Llandudno? But that's just what we did, and the venture gobbled up all my savings and bit into our earnings too. Eventually we had to admit defeat and sell at a great loss, but it says a lot for Dorothy and Bill that we always remained close friends. It was the most heartbreaking shock when, just before I went to the rehearsal for the 1974 Eurovision Song Contest, I switched on my Ansafone to hear Dorothy's sobbing voice tell me of Bill's sudden death during the night. He was one of the most remarkable people I have ever met, and I'm so glad that Dorothy is still part of my life.

That blasted dry-cleaning venture very nearly claimed another casualty – our marriage. My continual to-ing and fro-ing up north, on top of all my other travels and working commitments, meant that even my occasional weekend outings to the racecourse with Greville went by the board. Understandably, there was somebody else who was only too pleased to make sure he wasn't left alone. I can only blame myself for this '*amitié amoureuse*' (a lovely but untranslatable French expression) having blossomed in the first place. I was concentrating wholeheartedly on my work and hardly at all on Greville's life. I played straight into the hands of this pretty woman, whose sole interests seemed to be racing and Greville (I may have the order the wrong way round). After all I was nearing forty, we'd been married for twelve years and, although she also had a husband at the time and two very young children, she was ten years younger than I.

I think I became aware of her presence as a threat when we were over-frequent visitors to their home, and they to ours. Greville wasn't all that keen on opening his door, so this contrast was marked.

And whereas before he had been reluctant to go to night-clubs, I found we were going to them more and more often and getting to bed later. Then again, Greville and I had separate telephone numbers, and when his rang and I picked it up, more often than not the caller hung up. Occasionally she would admit who it was, saying she wanted to discuss 'betting figures'. I simmered for a while, then exploded and told her in no uncertain terms she should lay off my husband as she had a perfectly good one of her own.

After that, I took a deep breath and casually mentioned my doubts and fears to Greville. He roared with laughter, which reassured me not one bit. There were all the classic signs, and I didn't know how to cope. My mind said, 'Be sophisticated – play it cool', my nature wanted to rant and rave. Although I didn't share Greville's love of racing, my love for him never wavered and it was certainly not my pride alone that was hurt by this young woman's influence. My jealousy knew no bounds, and with it all shame vanished. In a blind rage one day, I drove off clutching a carving knife with the intention of slashing her car-tyres, but then I couldn't remember which was her car, and luckily my fury had subsided by the time I reached the road where the lady lived – otherwise this story might have a different ending.

This liaison lasted in varying degrees for three years or so, and caused a great deal of anguish all round, especially after this woman got divorced and I believe expected Greville to marry her. But she hadn't taken into consideration the incredible bond between him and myself, and those all-important holidays.

I have no time for women who say, 'My husband has always been faithful to me,' and in fact it is of no importance to me now, but it is only fair to Greville that I should add that he forever maintained that he did not have an affair with this girl. Moreover, I think Greville's sister, Norah, for whom I have great affection, would murder me if I did not make this point clear. All that matters to me is that, when it was over, we found that it had brought us closer together rather than separated us.

Eurovision
Song Contests

As I've already mentioned, my connection with the Eurovision Song Contest spanned fourteen years. I introduced this show four times between 1960 and 1974, when England played host, because each winning country took over the following year with their own hostesses.

It was late in 1959 when Tom Sloan, by this time Head of BBC Television Light Entertainment, called me to his office again. 'Catherine,' he said – Tom never called me Katie or even Kate – 'you've had a good deal of TV experience by now. I've heard you switch easily from English to French and Italian with the family, so . . .' he paused, 'I'm going to let you introduce the Eurovision Song Contest. It will be a big occasion, and we are going to hold it at the Royal Festival Hall.'

My ambition has never been the compulsive 'push everything and everybody out of the way' kind. If somebody was given a job I would have liked, my disappointment lasted overnight, if that; the next day I'd be off on another tangent. But the Eurovision Song Contest was a plum job I was delighted to get.

I was over the moon. But as all the preparations gathered momentum, journalists, radio presenters and big names from the pop world poured in from all over Europe and the Festival Hall stage became crowded on the first day of rehearsals, my feet felt increasingly colder. The atmosphere backstage at a Eurovision Song Contest may have been slightly less pressured in those early days, but it was always charged with electricity and high hopes although, apart from the odd flash of temperament, the general feeling was one of cordial *camaraderie*. By the time the hall was filling up on the night, I was in a tizz of terror, wishing to heavens I'd never heard of television, Tom Sloan and above all the Eurovision Song Contest.

I peeped through the curtains and picked out Greville in the middle of a smartly-dressed audience. His expression was tense. He was obviously suffering from nerves as well and was fiddling with his programme. By the end of the show there was no more programme, and around his shoes was a mountain of tiny paper flakes.

But now, suddenly, a fanfare sounded and I was pushed from behind with only one way to go – forward out onto the stage. I thought my knees would give way, my jaw was locked but, to my astonishment, I heard the right words coming out.

Things are always professionally geared to go right and the BBC is a past master on this score. This is unfortunate for me because I'm at my best when things go wrong, but luck was on my side that night. We were halfway through the voting procedure when suddenly there was a hiss from a musician in the orchestra below. Then, Eric Robinson, that kind teddy bear of a conductor, pointed to the board with his baton and mouthed, 'There's a mistake.' I turned, looked at the figures and saw nothing. At the best of times I can't add two and two but the speed of the voting was extremely confusing. All the same I heard myself say, 'We must stop for a moment – I'm sorry – but I think there's a mistake in the scoring!' And luckily, in a flash, Alfred Wurmser, that wonderful designer of the score board, had slotted in the amended number. I remember it was a 9, and we moved ahead on course again. A little later I lost the line to Venice, but I managed to retrieve it, and suddenly the show was over. France won, with Jacqueline Boyer singing a catchy song called 'Tom Pillibi', and I was given the kudos of having kept my head at a time when I was least likely to lose it. Life's funny, isn't it?

In 1963 the Eurovision Song Contest, to my mind, was bound to be a shambles. It was to be held in two studios simultaneously at the Television Centre. In one were the singers, the orchestra and half the audience; in the other was the scoreboard, scorers, me and the rest of the audience. By some miracle though, or perhaps it was good management, the whole evening went off remarkably smoothly.

This was the year that Nana Mouskouri caused a sensation by appearing in those now famous horn-rimmed spectacles, and she has looked through them successfully ever since. Esther Ofarim, with that perfectly-pitched voice, represented Switzerland – remember her with her husband and their 'Cinderella, Rockafella' hit from a few years later? Tanse Vise won for Holland that year and Ronnie Carroll lost, despite his charm and 'Say Wonderful Things'.

That evening ended somewhat abruptly for me when, at the end of the show, I had my dress swiftly peeled off me like a banana-skin. Millie Martin slipped into it to do a take-off of me in the studio next door in 'That was The Week That Was'!

A few months after this a letter arrived from Venice to tell me that I had been awarded the prize for European Radio and Television Personality of the Year: 'We voted for Catherine Boyle because of her multi-lingual abilities as demonstrated in many Eurovision products, notably Eurovision Song Contests. Also for her capacity to retain poise and elegance when technical emergencies arise, as they sometimes do in the complex processes of the Eurovision Network.'

It was a terrific prize to win and I was tickled pink, but what gave me the biggest thrill of all (apart from the star-studded company I was in) was that my name was up there on the red and white banners strung across many of the Venetian *calle*. Yves Montand was voted top light music singer; Joan Sutherland was their opera singer; that superb Italian comedian Walter Chiari was their comedy award; Kenneth More was named as the dramatic actor for his role in Terence Rattigan's *Heart To Heart*, as a first production in the International Theatre of the Air series; Caterina Valente carried off the international star accolade for her all-round talent; Spaniard Antonio was voted for his particular style of Spanish ballet dancing; and Zizi Jeanmaire with her superb silhouette, voice and smile was the Euro-premio in the *Chorus Girl* category, whatever that may mean!

Understandably it was difficult to gather all the winners together in the same place at the same time, so the actual presentation of the awards was fixed for the following year, 1965, to coincide with the 25th International Exhibition of Cinematographic Art on the Venice

Lido – it was a real glory and glamour occasion. In the same week, I was asked by the organizers of this event to introduce on Eurovision, from Venice itself, an International Light Music concert.

This, too, was a splendid occasion in a fairytale setting. Piazza San Marco and the Piazzetta were both floodlit, and on the Grand Canal, anchored opposite the Doge's Palace, was this enormous floating stage. Sparkingly-domed and garlanded with a million lights, it held a full orchestra, a handful of conductors who became increasingly temperamental as the evening wore on, the odd official, a miniature monitor screen – and me. Our only link with *terra firma* was a narrow wooden ramp, red-carpeted and precariously-balanced, far too flimsy for the artists teetering to and fro at their peril!

The actual production was bedlam, more than ever for me, used to the determination and discipline of the BBC schedules. I never did meet the producer (I gather he was stuck somewhere in the Doge's Palace); we never had a rehearsal, let alone a run-through; the running order was haphazard – I was told the name of the next singer while the previous one sang. Halfway through the show, a grubby scrap of paper informed me that we were going out live on radio, at the same time as television, and when I glanced at the monitor I noticed a thick wooden stake sliced me in half from top to toe on the screen. All the same, despite the chaos, it really was a night to remember.

We took over the Royal Albert Hall for the 1968 Eurovision Song Contest. This I felt was a wonderful idea – lots of space for both stage and audience. Barefooted Sandie Shaw had been the outright winner of the year before in Venice with her great hit 'Puppet On A String', and now Cliff Richard was carrying all our hopes with 'Congratulations' (Spain was to pip him at the post with 'Boom bang a bang', unfortunately). Cliff is wonderful to work with and I also had one of my favourite people directing, Stewart Morris. My dress was a glorious black velvet high-neck bare-backed one. From S.J. Phillips in Bond Street I'd borrowed a fabulous brooch; it was an enormous diamond spray with a large rose which trembled shimmeringly on its stalk as I moved.

So all in all I was very happy about everything and, despite the usual tensions, was out to enjoy this particular show in full. For some unknown reason, though, Tom was wandering around more than usual. He looked worried, so I went up to the office he'd set up in the Albert Hall. 'Anything wrong?' I asked Queenie.

'Not that I know of. What makes you think there is?'

'Just a feeling!'

Then Tom walked in, grinned at me rather wryly and closed the door behind him. 'Greville wasn't in very good form last night, was he?'

'I think he was a bit tired,' was my reply. Tom had come by for a drink, and I remembered that Greville had gone downstairs to see him off.

Then Tom dropped into his chair, rested his elbows on the desk and looked hard at me.

'Have you ever thought there might be someone else in Greville's life? Someone he might want to marry?' Suddenly I felt very sick. So this was it. I knew exactly who he meant. I wanted to ask what Greville had actually said to him, but couldn't.

I didn't want to go to pieces. Not just then. I had to hold tight. Why had he brought this up at this moment? Someone called me back to rehearsal; soaked in a cold sweat, I went. There were still twenty-four hours to go before the actual contest. I was numb.

Rehearsals over, I couldn't face going home. I wanted to be alone. I tied a scarf round my hair and crossed the road into the park. It was getting dark and drizzling. I can't remember much else. It was past eleven when I eventually turned up at the flat, and Greville appeared to be out of his mind with worry. I blurted out what Tom had said, and made every kind of wild accusation. He looked stunned, then heatedly denied everything. He exploded with rage against Tom for what he'd said, then gently tried to make me see reason, soothed me, told me that I had nothing to worry about.

I shall never quite understand why Tom said what he did, but you can imagine my shattered state of mind as I walked on to the stage of the Royal Albert Hall that night to introduce the 1968 Eurovision Song Contest.

The last Eurovision Song Contest that I introduced was in 1974 and it was, as were all the others for one reason or another, a stimulating and memorable experience. It was held at the Brighton Pavilion at the height of the terrorist campaign, which lent tension and a sense of drama to the occasion – James Bond films had nothing on those few days. Bullet-proof buses ferried us to and from the hotel and theatre, always using different routes. Only carefully-scrutinized badges allowed us in and out of anywhere. Closed-circuit television followed us mercilessly and, with repeated bomb scares, policemen with dogs trained to sniff out explosives seemed to be coming out of the woodwork.

Greville, who came down to Brighton with me for the four days, raised an eyebrow on discovering that our bedroom was sandwiched between the Israeli and Irish contestants, and accepted being banned from our bus after leaving his badge upstairs.

But it wasn't only the political climate that caused trouble that year. My dress played a big part. To begin with it was made in a glorious salmon-pink satin and was meant to be generously trimmed with matching ostrich-feathers. But ... the ostrich-feathers were delayed, and when they turned up at the eleventh hour they were a horrifying clashing bright purple! ! So, the night before transmission, there was Joyce Mortlock, head of BBC wardrobe, stirring a cauldron of ostrich-feather soup in an attempt to change their colour. I despaired and panicked as she kept fishing out tatty bits of 'black string' – but not she; she kept at it with dogged determination and, eventually, in the small hours of the morning and with the help of a hair-drier and wide-toothed comb, she achieved the impossible – a perfect match.

The next hitch came when I put the dress on. Due to some ghastly misunderstanding, it wouldn't even meet over my bust and my bra and pants showed through blatantly – the lines would have been picked up a thousand times worse on the screen. There was no alternative – I had to strip and be sewn into the dress. And so it was that, as I walked out in front of those 600-million-plus televiewers, not to mention the packed audience in the Brighton Pavilion, there was merely a layer of satin between us.

1974 was the year Abba won the contest with 'Waterloo' and exploded on to the pop scene. They were a friendly, blue-jeaned foursome who, at one rehearsal, merged in so well with the mêlée that Greville mistook Agnetha for a BBC barmaid and asked her to get him a drink – which she did with a beaming smile. But Olivia Newton-John was by far the prettiest girl amongst a gang of international good-lookers, and despite an indifferent song, she showed the tremendous appeal so evident in *Grease*. This was also the year that Terry Wogan charmed his way round Europe doing his first radio commentary on the show – what natural wit he has.

I don't know what I would have done without Pat Wilson. Unobtrusive, with a quiet sense of humour, this prodigious polyglot of the BBC was my pillar. We hardly left each other's side. This amazing man with ten fluent languages at the tip of his tongue took endless time and trouble making sure that not only was I phonetically correct in all my 'hellos' and 'goodbyes', but that I also had at least one more colloquial sentence to fall back on in every language involved on the programme.

I thrived on this kind of coaching, and must have been a reasonably successful pupil, because a few days after the contest, I was walking along Bond Street when a couple rushed up and regaled me with gibberish. When I looked blank, they looked surprised and broke into English, 'But you speak our language so well.' It was Finnish. Thanks to Pat's tutoring I really had bluffed my way through yet again.

Anguish

It was in 1969 that a travel agency invited me to go to Acapulco; the firm had a tie-up with a *TV Times* competition and suggested that I should go as a glorified courier to their winners. Greville, never one to stand in the way of anything I wanted to do, encouraged me to accept what sounded like a fabulous job.

Little did I think that it was going to trigger off the most turbulent phase of our marriage. But when an attractive married man with two children appeared against the romantic back-cloth of that Mexican playground, I fell for him hook, line and sinker, and it was obvious he felt the same way about me.

It could so easily have become and remained a classic 'away from home' escapade – something that neither of us went in for, incidentally – although he assured me his marriage was far from happy. But it didn't. Back in England our work brought us into ever closer contact with each other. I learnt a great deal from him in the journalistic field, and we succumbed to the excitements and fears of a secret affair.

I'm not going to try and make excuses for my behaviour, but it's only natural in retrospect for me to analyse the reasons for such blinding emotions. Then again, if reason had reigned I would surely have acted very differently – the last thing in the world I ever wanted to do was to hurt Greville and put my marriage in serious jeopardy.

Greville always maintained that the blame as well as the credit in a close relationship should always be shared by both partners – and I was probably still bruised deep down by his liaison even though it was well and truly a thing of the past. Perhaps I was also prey to the early mental and physical symptoms of the menopause – a time when nature herself tends to shove you around, and a time when a woman undoubtedly craves for the extra reassurance of her continued appeal to the opposite sex.

Who knows! Human nature can be so destructively complex at times. If only feelings could be compartmentalized and relationships could be sliced into tidy shapes, it would be so much easier. But they can't and don't, so eventually, when I couldn't sort anything out any more, I ran away – to be alone, to think.

I've tried to forget those nightmarish six months of trekking round Britain to fulfil professional engagments, with a smile on my face and a car laden with six suitcases and a small Yorkshire terrier in an egg-basket; of driving through an endless storm-tossed night to North Wales, where those wonderful Eastwoods gave me shelter and asked no questions; and finally sinking into a basement flat in Pimlico, where having to look after one small dog was the only thing that kept me going.

It had taken me less than twenty-four hours away from Greville to realize I had no choice to make. I used a simple but effective method to decide, and I only wish I'd thought of it a great deal sooner. I just imagined the two men in a near fatal car-crash, rushed to hospitals at opposite sides of the city. My heart froze but I forgot everything but Greville. However, though I had no further doubts, the choice was now up to Greville.

I can't possibly go into the details of all the soul-searching and unhappiness during that interminable June to December. I dragged myself out to work, then sat alone indoors for hours poring over and trying to solve the problems of readers of my 'Dear Katie' page in the *TV Times*. Already in the depths of despair, I was driven mad every day by the constant drilling of workmen demolishing houses nearby. By night I was scared rigid by the scuffling, squeaking and jumping out from cupboards of hundreds of mice made homeless by the demolition. To make matters worse, Tessa, my Yorkie, never gave up chasing the mice and expected praise when she killed. So if I dropped off to sleep, she'd jump up on the bed and drop her latest soggy victim on my face.

When I could stand it no longer I called the Rentokil men in, but I had to telephone Greville to ask him if he'd have Tessa for a few days. Of course he agreed but he rang me to say she'd slept like a dead dog for forty-eight hours and he was loath to let me have this still-exhausted scrap back. She stayed for a few more days of rest with him, then he brought her round to me.

This wasn't the first time Greville and I had been in touch with each other since I'd left home. From the very first day I'd always told our housekeeper, Teresa, of my whereabouts for one reason or another and she had been a permanent link between us – and there's no doubt whatsoever that our mutual caring never stopped. But after Tessa had turned mouse-hunter, we talked more and more often.

He came to dinner in my little warren; I went home to spend the evening with him. The time came round when we usually booked our holiday – he brought up the subject. A few days later he telephoned to say he'd booked the same room we'd had before in Kenya, at Tradewinds on Diani Beach south of Mombasa. 'I think it's wiser to do this – they get very booked up and we can always cancel nearer the time,' were his words.

My heart missed a beat.

There was another month to go before Christmas by now. Christmas lists had to be made up; we made them up together. A week later when I was at home with him for dinner I had a wretched cold and it was raining outside and bitterly windy. He suggested that I should stay overnight; we talked until dawn, then I left. A few hours later, with suitcases packed and a car heavily-laden, I drove back again to Cranmer Court. With my heart in my mouth I rang my front-door bell. The door opened, Greville's arms went round me and I was home – to stay.

The fact that there were no young children, other duties or 'convenience' reasons to bring us back together again proved to us both that we were necessary to each other. But though our traumas definitely brought, and kept, us closer than we'd ever been before,' I would never recommend extra-marital affairs. The pain caused to everyone involved is far too high a price to pay for fleeting excitement.

Yes, Greville welcomed me back with a heart full of love. The aftermaths were occasional waves of sadness and silence, but very few recriminations. Those were swept away, once and forever, in the anticipation and preparations for this all-important healing holiday.

Away from everything and everybody we re-found each other and the weeks flew by. We shared a tremendous sense of relief at being together again, and just as he looked to me to restore his self-confidence, when I woke up at night in a cold sweat thinking of what I'd nearly thrown away, Greville's hand reached out to reassure me.

When we boarded the plane back to England there was no doubt whatsoever that our relationship had gained a new dimension in love and understanding. The next two years consolidated these feelings. We spoke often and enthusiastically about the time that lay ahead and began, at last, to look forward to growing old together.

January 1976 saw us back at Tradewinds. This we knew was going to be the best holiday ever. Even the small brown-and-white beach dog, Girlie, who had adopted us the year before, would stay with nobody else and hadn't been seen for three whole months, was waiting faithfully for us. We immediately had her inoculated against rabies and began making plans to take her back to England with us in February.

We didn't even have to unwind this time. The same beachboys laid out our chairs by the swimming-pool, the friendly Swahili greeting, '*Jambo, Habari?*' came from all the familiar faces, and the smooth, bleached sands stretched out for miles on our morning walks.

Four blissful days went by, and on the fifth morning Greville hugged me before he left the bedroom. 'Don't be long, my darling.'

'Of course not,' I said. 'I'll just put on this new tanning-lotion I want to try.' And I watched him leave with Girlie at his heels.

It seemed only seconds later that I heard screams coming from the direction of the swimming-pool, then running footsteps under my window and cries of 'Mrs Baylis, Mrs Baylis come quickly, your husband has had a dreadful accident.'

I fled down the stairs and along the path. There, with his arms round two men's shoulders, Greville was being dragged, stumbling towards the car park. Blood was pouring from his left thigh and there was a red trail leading back to the swimming-pool.

His face was ashen but all he kept saying was. 'Oh! darling, I've ruined our holiday!'

It was Anne Flanagan who had run to call me, and now it was her husband Alan, an engineer with East African Airways, who, with the Hotel Manager, was heaving my heavily-built husband into the back of a small car. He tied his shirt round Greville's leg but, in seconds, the blood was soaking through onto the thick foam-rubber cushion. I slid into the front seat next to Alan and we set off towards Mombasa. Although the road was good those twenty odd miles went on forever. The blood-stain spread wider and wider, Greville's face was painfully drawn and parchment pale. I reached back and held his hand.

'What happened exactly?' I felt it might help to keep him talking.

'Well, it sounds so ridiculous. I was walking along the side of the swimming-pool – obviously a bit too close to the edge. I turned back and waved hello to one of the beachboys, missed my footing and fell into the shallow end. As I went down I must have gashed my thigh on the stone ledge.'

Then he started worrying about Girlie. 'I hope she doesn't think that we've let her down and left her again.'

'No, no, darling, I'm sure she doesn't. She'll wait patiently by our room. Just let's concentrate on you now.' I looked at Alan. His expression was grim.

As we approached the ferry one boat was just leaving. I threw myself out of the car towards the man in charge. He must have sensed my panic because the boat back-pedalled so that we could squeeze our car aboard. By the time we reached the doctor's office, Greville was fighting hard to stay conscious. He leant heavily on Alan and me as we dragged him up some stairs to the waiting-room.

It was still early morning and the doctor hadn't arrived, but the nurse agreed to let us into the surgery. It was Alan though who manœuvred Greville's near dead-weight onto the high examination bed. The nurse appeared totally uninterested. She sifted through a pile of mail, dropped a letter, picked it up off the floor then, without washing her hands, sauntered over to Greville and prodded round the now uncovered wound.

I gasped at the sight. It was a deep five- or six-inch-long gaping mass of jagged flesh, and the blood was still slowly pumping through this red, raw pulp.

I wanted to strangle the nurse for being what I felt was completely indifferent – and when she said, 'Oh, people don't bleed to death so easily,' I could only turn away.

If it hadn't been for Alan's soothing arm round my shoulders I'd have been hysterical. He led me out onto the verandah. I leant on the railings and saw, just below, a tiny emaciated kitten stagger weakly under the wheels of a car. I turned back into the surgery. By now Greville was lying back on the bed. His closed eyes were sunk deep into their dark sockets. I was sure he was dying. I felt so desperately frightened.

It was like being in a nightmare where everything was happening in slow motion, and I was helpless.

Eventually the doctor arrived. The relief was tremendous, but I was defeated immediately. He was so young and announced cheerfully that Greville was his very first patient on his very first day in practice. I could only scream inside when he just looked at the wound, sprinkled some white powder on it and told the nurse to bandage it. I felt sure Greville needed at least something for the shock he'd had but the doctor just pooh-poohed such an idea. 'See you tomorrow morning – same time!' was all he said. I felt far from reassured.

The terrible drives to and from Mombasa and this 'treatment' were a continuing nightmare over the next four days. Girlie, incidentally, came too; she seemed to understand we were very worried, and behaved impeccably.

Back at the hotel, Greville was always in dreadful pain; the doctor didn't give him pain-killers – I did. Blood seeped non-stop through the dressings and I could see no improvement. Then on the fifth morning when the doctor took off the bandages, the wound had developed an enormous haematoma – a raised, banana-thick blood-blister.

'We *must* have a second opinion!' I tried hard to sound calm.

Thank God the doctor agreed. He telephoned the surgeon Declan O'Keefe; luckily he was in his office and we went round immediately. I trusted the tall and reassuring Mr O'Keefe on sight. He took one look at Greville's thigh and insisted on operating within the hour to remove the haematoma and stitch up the wound. At last something was being done!

Everyone at the Katherine Bibby Hospital, Mombasa, was kindness itself. Even the Matron loved dogs and allowed Girlie to sit in her air-conditioned office while I saw Greville settled into his room. But somehow I just couldn't shake off a chilling fear. While the operation was in progress, I sat with Girlie in the hospital gardens looking across the sea; the warm trade winds blew in my face, but my heart was gripped in a cold vice of terror. Tears I couldn't stop fell onto Girlie's coat; she looked up, her brown eyes full of love, trying to comfort me.

I kept telling myself that this was a natural reaction of relief after the traumas of the past days. But even after the operation, when Greville was quietly sleeping and Mr O'Keefe had seen me off and reassured me, I drove back to the hotel with a nagging, sickening premonition that something dreadful was still going to happen.

It was silly, however, because forty-eight hours later I collected Greville from the hospital and together we drove back to Tradewinds.

It was 10 February 1976. We still had ten days to go before we flew back home. Not long enough really for Greville to convalesce completely, but we were determined to enjoy them. I found it strange though, for someone who was usually a sun-worshipper and a great holiday reader, that Greville didn't want to sunbathe and lost all interest in books. But he was so patient and never grumbled once about his obvious discomfort.

We would sit for hours on our balcony, him puffing vaguely on a cigar, me vaguely embroidering – just chatting, or listening to the palms and looking out to sea.

'How am I looking?' he'd ask.

'A bit drawn, darling,' I'd say, 'but a lot better than yesterday.'

Then, one evening, he looked across at me. There was infinite sadness in his eyes. 'I don't think I'm long for this world, my darling.'

It was a gentle whisper. Suddenly on that hot tropical evening I felt ice-cold.

He went on, 'Even if I do die, we've been very lucky, haven't we? We've had a fantastic innings together. Twenty-four years really. And all things considering, ours has been a wonderful marriage, you know!' I couldn't speak. I just reached out for his hand, and we sat in silence, our thoughts only for each other, feeling like two frightened children.

Our journey home worried us. Although Girlie's documents had come through, she wasn't allowed on the small Mombasa to Nairobi plane. Greville persuaded me he'd be all right to make that short trip alone and I set off on the overnight train with a very happy dog. Girlie took to travelling like the proverbial duck to water. She and I gazed out of the window as the barren African landscape darkened with the night, then lit up eerily under a full moon. Later we fell into a deep sleep, sharing, side by side, the hard narrow bed.

The Flanagans met us at dawn and we were all at the airport to greet Greville. He was limping slightly, but assured us he'd be fine to travel on to London after a good sleep. I changed the dressing on his leg before we boarded the plane. By now the wound looked healthy and was healing well. All the same, after a few hours in the air, he appeared to be in considerable pain.

That journey seemed endless. The fact that Greville never once complained worried me stiff. Like most men he was usually convinced that a sore throat spelt cancer and a cold, incipient pneumonia. Once back at Gatwick, late at night, he wouldn't leave until we'd seen Girlie was all right, and made sure the car from the quarantine kennels was on its way to collect her.

It was in the early hours of Sunday, 22 February that Greville and I at last slept in our own home. A fitful sleep though – we kept waking up: 'I wonder how Girlie's getting on?'

'Is your leg still hurting?'

'It's throbbing a bit, but not really painful. I wish you didn't have to leave tomorrow!'

I was due in Plymouth for a personal appearance, then had to travel straight on to Cardiff. I dreaded leaving Greville that evening, and clung to him. He looked dreadfully tired.

'Don't you worry. The doctor says I'm fine. He's coming again tomorrow.'

He telephoned me after the doctor's visit, and sounded very cheerful. 'There's nothing to worry about at all. The wound is going along fine, and he says I'll live!'

'Oh! please don't joke about such a thing!' I was over-reacting, but Greville laughed.

It was now Wednesday. The journey across country to Cardiff had been chaotic. I'd even been put on the wrong train when I'd changed. The telephone was ringing when I got to my room.

'Hello darling. I just wanted to hear your voice. Are you all right?'

'Yes, fine, but ...' (I told him of my adventures).

It was six p.m., and jet-lag was really catching up on me. I hadn't had a chance to sleep it off. I said I'd have an early night, get to bed and wade through all the mail I still hadn't read.

'That's a good idea. I'll call you again about eight o'clock.'

We talked then, and again at 9.30 – we always seemed to have so much to say.

'I think I'll turn off the light soon. Will you go to bed early too?'

'Yes, but I'll probably watch a bit of boxing first ... I was thinking, aren't we lucky to have each other?'

'Oh! so very lucky, and think of all the years we still have together. Isn't it wonderful?'

'We're more in love than ever before, aren't we?'

'Yes, we really are.'

I put out the light and cuddled down with those loving words in my heart.

The telephone rang. Short, persistent rings nagged me out of the deepest sleep.

I looked at my little clock. It glowed 4.30 a.m. Where was I? I couldn't remember. The bell shrilled again. There must be some mistake. I groped vaguely towards the bell – I couldn't find the light.

'Yes,' I growled.

'Is that Miss Boyle?' I'd never heard the voice before.

'Yes,' I snapped, impatiently this time.

'I have some bad news for you – your husband is dead!'

171

I remember nothing. Teresa, our housekeeper, who was standing next to that heartless doctor, says my screams through the telephone were blood-curdling.

The shock was shattering. I found the light switch at last, but the small room was suddenly hostile. I was suffocating. I think I just sat there, but I must have telephoned Peter Cattle's room. Peter has been a very dear friend for many years, ever since his days as deputy editor of the *Sunday Graphic*. He was now in charge of public relations for Pye/Ekco so we were working together there in Cardiff. How kind he was that terrible night. I can still see him sitting on the edge of my bed making enquiries about trains to London. Then, somehow, we were on a station together. As the train drew out he was on the platform, waving. I noticed he still had on his pyjama trousers under his overcoat. The rhythm of the train repeated 'Greville, Greville' for hours on end. A man handed me his handkerchief. Did I return it? I don't know. Then, at last, London. Bunny Lewis, my faithful agent, was waiting for me. He tucked his arm under mine. He said nothing – neither could I.

The billboards seemed to have nothing to do with me. They read, 'Katie Boyle's husband dies'; 'Katie Boyle a widow.' Yes, that was me – I was a widow.

We reached the flat at last. I think I saw Teresa and Joanie as I fled past the kitchen, down the corridor to the bedroom. This time I do remember screaming. Greville, still so tanned, looked peacefully asleep. His face, his hands, were only just cooling – the firm skin was still soft and sweet-smelling. As I fell on his chest, his last breath exhaled into my tears. No, this wasn't a dead man. It couldn't be. This was a wicked, sick joke they were playing. I touched his hair, kissed his eyes, his lips, his hands. This wasn't happening – why couldn't I wake him up?

'Oh, please, Greville, wake up! *Please!*'

The rest is blurred. Door-bells rang, people I'd never seen came and went. Friends, oh yes, wonderful friends rallied round me.

Flowers kept arriving. I wished they wouldn't. I was a widow, not a bride. Then they closed the drawing-room door. Why? They wouldn't let me out. The front door slammed. I had to go – I ran on to the landing – the lift was leaving. Oh! no! Back in the flat,

I flew to the bedroom. The bed was empty, Greville was gone, they'd taken him away – but they couldn't do that. I just knew he wasn't dead. What could I do?

His pyjama-jacket lay limply on the sheets. At least that they wouldn't have. I clung to it. Hours dragged by. It was dark now. Teresa, red-eyed and exhausted, was persuading me into bed. I had to wear that jacket. It smelt of him. I had to lie where he had been, hug his pillows – I couldn't move – I wouldn't. None of this was really happening; tomorrow I'd wake up and everything would be all right again.

Of course it wasn't. If anything it was even worse. After a deep sleep I was fully conscious, agonizingly aware of the dreadful tragedy. Greville was killed by a massive coronary thrombosis – that scourge as endemic to this age as smallpox was to the fourteenth century.

It's a bitter indictment against this age too that I was immediately offered pills to dull my despair. I refused them all, for to camouflage my emotions, even on the day of his funeral, I felt would be unworthy of Greville, as well as make it worse for me later.

Bunny Lewis took complete charge of all the immediate arrangements. I don't know what I could have done without him. Margherita and Enrico flew over from Switzerland at once. They loved Greville dearly and were stunned too. But Margherita insisted on the Saturday after Greville had died on the Wednesday/Thursday night, that I still do my long-standing programme on BBC Radio 2, 'Pop Over Europe'. I remember nothing of that morning except that the producer Steve Allen and engineer Ray Hall, dear friends both of them, were silently understanding.

Then, four days after the funeral, I decided I had to honour my contract with Woolworth's. Nine whole weeks of a show in a different town every single night, except for Sundays. The effort of travelling non-stop to all the places, as well as visiting Girlie in the quarantine kennels, drained all the physical energy from me. What carried me through emotionally was the warmth of the audiences. Each one seemed to consist of individuals who felt my anguish and willed me to get through the show. The models were also towers of strength. In fact to everyone involved in that painful marathon

I shall always be eternally grateful. Looking back on it all now, perhaps it even saved my sanity.

My work was so pressurized for weeks on end that only several months after Greville's death did I begin to realize just how much loneliness, how much vulnerability, is welded into that word 'widow'. The difference between organizing and getting on with every day details when Greville was in the background was enormous in comparison to coping alone. But it was a relief and a comfort to telephone Teresa every night and morning and go back home to her on Sundays. She – as well as Joan – had been with us for many years, and were closely involved in our highs and lows. Now they were determined to do all they could, despite their own shock and grief, to help me.

A Guiding
Hand

It may seem odd, but from the very first moments, when the smithereens of my world threatened to submerge me, I was aware of the importance of words. To begin with there were the letters. They poured in. I would never have believed they could have been of such comfort. But they were. Whether they came from friends, acquaintances or strangers, their warmth, the knowledge that people cared enough to write, was incredibly reassuring.

I am also deeply grateful to the many readers of my 'Dear Katie' page who never stopped bringing me their problems when I needed so desperately to escape from my own unhappiness. Over the ten years I've been with the *TV Times* I've received over a million letters, and although I like to feel I've been able to help at times, I know I've been taught a great deal about life in exchange – never more so than during that dreadful year.

All those words I read over and over again, and took comfort from them when I needed it so badly. But I think the ones which helped me most to survive instant widowhood are these, written by Canon Scott Holland, who was an eminent theologian during Queen Victoria's reign. I believe them implicitly:

Death is nothing at all – I have only slipped away into the next room. I am I, and you are you. Whatever we were to each other, that we still are. Call me by my old familiar name, speak to me in the easy way which you always used. Wear no forced air of solemnity or sorrow. Laugh as we always laughed at the little jokes we enjoyed together. Play, smile, think of me, pray for me. Let my name be ever the household word that it always was. Let it be spoken without effect, without the ghost of a shadow on it. Life means all that it ever meant. It is the same as it ever was. There is absolutely unbroken continuity. What is this death but a negligible accident? Why should I be out of mind because I am out of sight? I am waiting for you – for an interval – somewhere very near just around the corner. All is well.

About two months after Greville died, I was reading these lines yet again and twiddling my wedding rings. Greville wore his wedding ring, with his signet ring, on his little finger. When he died I took it off, and put it on next to my own. It had slipped on very easily, but now, somehow, it looked smaller.

I tested my engagement ring. This came off as usual with a slight lift, and the wedding one swivelled around just as it had always done. But there was no doubt that Greville's ring had definitely shrunk.

To confirm what I could see, I washed my hands and tried to coax the ring off a well-soaped finger. Then I tried the old trick of threading a piece of string under it. But no – it resisted all attempts to remove it! A tingle ran down my spine. The silence of death, that sudden breakdown of all obvious communication, I had found to be one of the most anguishing parts of widowhood. Now, suddenly, it was broken by this symbolic gold circle. I felt Greville had spoken as lovingly and more loudly than with words.

I do fervently believe in the continuity of life to life through death. And I am equally certain that the bridge between the two worlds is built on 'love'. I'm well aware that I am laughed at both publicly and privately for my beliefs, and I would never try to influence those people. On the other hand, so many things have happened to me, so often, which make me quite sure that they, and their repetition, go way beyond coincidence.

After all why should anyone be so conceited as to feel that we are the ultimate in knowledge and experience? Of one thing I am certain: without my convictions I doubt whether I would have had the resilience to bounce back from some of the knocks I've had.

Like so many people whose loved ones have died I did go to see a medium. A close friend, Myrtle Winstone, had been to see one because she had hoped to contact her father. During the session the medium had said someone with the initial G, who had died suddenly very recently, was most anxious to send all his love to his wife, and would Myrtle please tell her that it was extremely lucky that they had travelled back from their holiday together, because if he had stayed, it would still have happened over in Africa. Greville and I had indeed discussed the possibility of him staying on at Tradewinds without me to gain a little more strength, but dismissed the idea very quickly, and I had mentioned it to no one.

Anyway, I hadn't spoken to Myrtle since Greville's death, so neither she, and certainly not the medium, could possibly have known that there was any such question. It was because of this incident that I felt this woman was the right medium for me. I'm very wary and watchful for the 'wrong' ones. There is so much scope for quackery in this field.

Despite my booking an appointment in another name, wearing dark glasses, a headscarf and no make-up, as soon as I said 'Hello', the medium recognized me.

'Your voice gives you away,' she said at once. 'So it's no good pretending I haven't read about your sad news.' I liked her frankness.

Hers is a pleasant, bright room, overlooking lots of trees. There was no drawing of curtains or phoney solemnity. We simply sat in two armchairs on opposite sides of the fireplace. My emotions were running very high. I wasn't prepared to rely on my memory, so I had taken along a pad and a pen, and as she spoke I scribbled down everything she said.

As anyone who has been to a medium knows, there is always a lot of what I call 'padding' – things that are said which are a comfort, but could easily be attributed to most people in similar circumstances. Things like, 'He loves you so dearly', 'He was desperately sorry to leave you' etc. But gradually, that afternoon, Greville's whole personality took shape.

The medium referred to private conversations between the two of us which she could never have imagined. She repeated virtually verbatim our conversation when Greville had tried to tell me he felt he would soon die, and she mentioned that this took place on a bedroom balcony very near the sea.

177

When I told her how much I regretted not having a record of his voice, she immediately reminded me that I had indeed an Ansafone tape – something I had completely forgotten. She then got the name, which she was unable to pronounce, of my first Italian love. She told me of his violent death by a firing-squad, and added that he was now handing over my care to Greville. This impressed me tremendously, because Franco *had* been executed so many years ago. Greville seemed determined to establish his identity through the medium. She mentioned a small, square gold frame in which I keep my favourite snapshot of him; she said it had originally been used for a photograph of his two grandchildren, and I'd switched pictures – indeed I had.

As I was sitting there neither 'feeling' nor 'seeing' anything in the way of a presence, I asked her how, or from what, did she interpret her 'messages'. 'I can't describe exactly – colours, vibrations, sounds – I don't know. But I know Greville is going towards you right now.' I felt nothing at all.

'He loves Tessa, doesn't he? Look!' I glanced down at the egg basket in which my Yorkie had been curled, sound asleep. Now she was gazing up into space, as far as I could make out. Then she sat bolt upright, her ears went up and down in greeting, and her tongue shot in and out like an anteater's. She always 'throws' kisses. Suddenly she flung herself on her back, in her basket, as she had always done when Greville approached her, waving her front paw and asking to have her tummy rubbed – and still that tongue shot in and out as if to kiss his hand.

I choked back the tears. What possible explanation could there be for her behaviour? I'm quite sure that she was aware of something which escaped me.

When I got home, I went over and over the notes I'd made during my time with the medium. I believe I was totally detached, but try as I might there were many points which were beyond all logic. Even now, nearly four years later, I have those scribbled pages here in front of me, and I am still at a loss for any reasonable explanation. I did go and see her two or three more times. She tended to be repetitive, but always equally convincing. Then, gradually I felt I was in need of her help no longer. The link between Greville and myself had become a direct one. I only had to ask him and in some strange but very definite way he was there.

My first experience of this came about in such a mundane manner. About four months after his death, I faced a hectic day full of business appointments. As usual, driving around London, I just hoped I'd find conveniently-placed parking-spaces. Thinking of Greville I mouthed rather vaguely, 'I wish you'd help me, darling.'

Near the first address there was a meter. 'That was lucky, wasn't it?' I murmured.

As I pulled out to go to the next rendezvous, I thought, 'Let's see, darling, if luck is still with me!' Then I smiled for being so silly. But ... sure enough there was a space.

The third free meter really surprised me, and as I drove towards my fourth appointment, I said, 'I wonder if you really are helping me, Greville? I'd love to believe you were!' I felt strangely confident – but, as I approached the door of H.L. Puckle's former offices in Chandos Street, W1, cars packed both sides of the road. Not a hope. I was just going to put my foot down and try elsewhere when an engine started up, and a Jaguar driver beckoned me into the space he was leaving. I backed in, and was about to say 'Thank you, darling,' when my eyes fell on the initials of the Rover in front of me – G.P.B. They were Greville's initials!!

I was up Puckle's stairs in a flash, and down again pulling David Jacques with me. 'There, look – what are those initials?' I cried, showing him the car. 'Greville's initials,' he replied, slightly bewildered, but he is now my willing witness to this story.

Since then I have always found a parking-space whenever I've asked Greville to help me, and he also comes to the aid of a number of my friends in need. One of them in particular, Ann Calvert, can vouch for many such experiences. I can't explain it, but I must regard this welcome, practical, tangible help as an everyday link between Greville and myself which has continued ever since I became aware of it back in 1976.

Although I haven't mentioned my mother for a good many pages, this doesn't mean that she wasn't always very close to Greville and myself. Happily married, since the early fifties, to Patrick Boyle (who succeeded the well-loved Admiral 'Ginger' Boyle as Earl of

Cork and Orrery), they lived just outside Petworth in a picture-book cottage, and were both very much a part of our lives. Mama had always wanted a son, and Greville, very affectionate and protective towards her, had filled this gap. I sometimes wondered whether she didn't love him even more than she did me.

Unfortunately, when still in her early sixties, Mama started to develop arteriosclerosis. Her mind gradually became a little muddled, and above all her memory blurred. She recognized us all less and less, and her powers of speech and movement deteriorated to virtually nothing. Eventually, and regretfully, Patrick had no alternative but to entrust her to the wonderful care of the White-hanger Nursing-Home, just outside Haslemere. It was there that she spent the last five years of her life. Her charm never left her, she was forever smiling, and her snow-white hair framed her still pretty face. I felt, though, that our visits served to distress her and raise question-marks, so I went down to see her very rarely.

Although I knew she spent most of her time in a twilight world, three months after Greville's death I did go down to Whitehanger. I held her listless hand and, looking into her large, vacant eyes, said: 'Mama darling, I want you to know that Greville died suddenly a little while ago.'

I expected no reaction at all. Instead her eyes immediately focused on mine, and for the first time in more than a year she spoke intelligibly. 'Oh, no! How dreadful! My poor darling!' Both her hands clasped mine firmly.

Then she turned her head, looked up between us and smiled in happy recognition. 'But look, Catherine, it's all right! It's all right! He's here – Greville's here with us!'

I, too, turned, saw nothing and looked back at her. The face so lively a second ago had gone blank again, and her hands had fallen limply away from mine. Early on 26 February 1978 – on, incredibly, the very same date and at exactly the same hour as Greville two years before – Mama died quietly in her sleep.

Her funeral was private; it was drizzling steadily. Only Patrick and I watched as the tiny coffin, covered by his Heraldic banner, was carried into the bare chapel. The priest read the words of Canon Scott Holland. I didn't feel she was alone at all, and neither were we.

The longer I live, the deeper my personal philosophy becomes. It is, that if we can accept that men can walk on the moon, communicating with others hundreds of thousands of miles away with no visible link; watch television programmes, projected via satellites from that moon as well as from other parts of the world; carry wireless transistors which bring sounds loud and clear through the air; accept that all forms of energy must have existed in the universe long before they were harnessed by scientific minds; if we accept these things, and realize that we would probably have been burnt at the stake for predicting their existence even a mere century or two ago, then why should we not be prepared to admit the possible existence of other power sources? Healing and paranormal waves are amongst many others yet to be revealed and acknowledged in full.

I first came across a faith healer when Greville was still alive and I was doing a BBC radio programme called *Melody Fare*. I played records during most of the show, but also had an out-and-about spot. One day I decided to investigate judo, so Patience Bunting and I set off to meet Senta Yamada, a Japanese black belt, at a judo school in Stoke Newington. We were heavily laden with a tape-recorder and producer Harry Rogers's words rang in our ears: 'Remember this isn't television, so bring back some good sound effects.' Harry needn't have worried: my devotion to duty was such that, as Mr Yamada flung me through the air, I clutched my mike and, instead of landing on my forearms, my neck hit the ground first with a loud crack and a yelp from me for the microphone. The pain was acute but seemed to wear off. About ten days later, however, in the middle of the night I woke up in agony. I could turn neither left nor right.

There followed the most excruciatingly painful two months. I was taken from doctor to specialist, from osteopath to chiropractor and finally to an orthopaedic surgeon who manipulated me under anaesthetic – but even he was unable to help. Eventually I lay back in a nursing home learning to enjoy my daily dose of morphine, the only thing which gave me any relief from the pain. Under its effect I even agreed to be photographed for a newspaper – and it was this picture of me (humorously placed above an advertisement for tomb-stones) that brought a shoal of letters. They all said that, if I'd only go and see a faith healer called Edward Fricker, I'd be cured and completely out of pain. Each letter told a personal story of some 'miracle' this man had performed. I was grateful, of course, but did little except show the letters to the surgeon and matron, then swallow another morphine tablet. Eventually, still wearing a surgical collar and with little or no feeling in my left arm and hand, I was driven home by Greville.

After only a few hours I was crying out in such agony that he decided, much against my will, to telephone this Mr Fricker for an appointment. 'He can't possibly hurt you by laying on his hands, and he might just help,' were his words.

I felt Mr Fricker must be a quack and would achieve nothing, but was feeling too weak to object, so I arrived at his 'office' in a hostile frame of mind. Ted Fricker, a solidly built man, beamed at me from behind horn-rimmed glasses.

'You don't think much of me,' he stated. I shook my head.

'You have no faith.'

'Oh, yes, I believe in God. But not in you!'

He went on smiling and said, 'Oh, well, the Guvnor's got enough faith for us all.' Then he went behind a screen, washed his hands and, coming out, put on a Beatles' record. He turned it up too loud and I raised an eyebrow at Greville, who was sitting a few yards away from me. Fricker then took my limp left arm.

'You have two discs out of place in your neck,' he said. I'd been told this by the hospital. 'Don't worry, we'll soon put them right.'

I found his confidence irritating. His hands touched the back of my neck – they felt like warm pads, and became warmer as he vibrated just where it hurt most. He took my arm and rubbed it from shoulder to finger-tips. The warmth was very soothing. He went back to my neck again. After three or four minutes, the pain seemed to have seeped away completely, leaving me very near to tears of relief. I couldn't believe what was happening.

I heard Ted say, 'Go and get hold of your husband's hand.'

'But I can't ...,' I began.

'Oh, yes, you can.'

I walked over to Greville and I could indeed move my hand again and feel his. Although completely free of pain now, I was still very suspicious.

'You are obviously an excellent hypnotist,' I conceded, 'but how long will this effect last?'

Poor man, he couldn't win with me, but he remained unruffled and smiling: 'You go off to see your doctors. There's nothing wrong with you any more. You'll probably just have to come back two or three more times for me to get that hand and arm stronger. But that's all.'

And that *was* all.

This happened twelve years ago and since then I have only had a frozen shoulder and a hereditary problem in my lower back that Ted hasn't been able to put right. Only recently I was nearly killed in a crash: my car skidded on a patch of black ice and ended up embedded in a ditch. Despite my wearing a seat-belt, I suffered a severe whiplash in my neck. Once again I rushed to Ted Fricker and, as I knew they would, his healing hands broke through the muscle spasm and saved me from endless pain that no conventional practitioner could have eased. Far from being a quack, Ted is a kind man with a great gift of healing. After these personal experiences, plus having witnessed so many other incidents, how can I not keep an open mind towards what is luckily being regarded less disparagingly every year as 'fringe medicine'?

I know that some people will be very sceptical about all this, but I have always believed in the maxim 'speak as you find'. I have felt this to be true from the time that I first came into contact with well-known people. I had expected to meet their media-created images; instead, more often than not, I discovered a very different personality. A typical case in point is Lady Falkender. Quite frankly, from afar and in print, Marcia Falkender scared me. But when our paths crossed, my opinion changed abruptly.

I was introducing the annual Pye TV Awards, and we were both attending the luncheon prior to the presentation at the Dorchester Hotel. At the time, I was on the look-out for a large-print typewriter so that I could prepare my script cards to read at a glance, without using my glasses. When I mentioned this over the luncheon, Jimmy

Green, television critic of the *Evening News*, and a buddy of mine for many years, piped up: 'That's the person to help you,' nodding over at Lady Falkender.

My need was greater than my fear of the lady, so I went over to the top table and leant across towards her. She was extremely helpful but I thanked her too exuberantly. With a Latin wave of my arms, I knocked a bottle of red wine into her lap. 'Counteract it,' was my first thought, but there was no white wine within reach (this works every time), so in panic I grabbed a jug of well-iced water to dilute the danger, and poured the whole lot onto an already very damp Lady Falkender. After a second's astonished silence, she and her sister Peggy Field, who was sitting next to her, burst into peals of laughter. Unfortunately, I couldn't linger because my cue came to go on stage. With barely time to throw a most inadequate, 'You'll dry off soon,' over my shoulder, I hurried away, but when I reached the stage, I could see that delightful pair of sisters still giggling helplessly.

As well as enjoying her marked sense of humour and of the ridiculous, I find the supposedly-fearsome Marcia Falkender to be one of the kindest, most helpful of people and great company to be with.

Another lady who has often, quite wrongly, been shown by the media as a sad grey mouse of a woman is Lady Wilson, Sir Harold's wife. We sat near each other at the twenty-first anniversary of the Woman of the Year Luncheon at the Savoy. (Incidentally, this was founded by the Marchioness of Lothian in aid of the Greater London Fund for the Blind; how ironic that Lady Lothian herself should have had to have an eye removed.)

Mary Wilson and I talked about many things and found each other on very much the same wave-length. One special point of contact we shared was the emotional anguish of battling with bereavement. On the eve of an election campaign, a close friend of hers died suddenly – I well remember those pictures in the press attributing her unhappy expression to everything but the truth. The more we talked, the more I realized that Mary Wilson, far from being a mouse-like creature, was someone with great depth of feeling, tremendous guts, gentle understanding and warmth. Everyone who enjoys her poems must know this, and I wasn't the least bit surprised when through the post, a day or two later, her poem about bereavement arrived – just as she'd promised it would at that luncheon.

I knew I would have to leave our large flat in Cranmer Court, where we lived for over twenty years, but a whole year passed before I was able to make such a decision. During that time, I took every job Bunny Lewis suggested. If I went to bed exhausted, I slept. In the morning (always the worst time) I had to start off too early to think of anything else.

Eventually I put the flat on the market, and tried to ignore what leaving it would involve. It was a chaotic, badly-planned move. Without Teresa and Joanie, I would never have made it. I was packing and still working non-stop, while the builders took an interminable muddled time to make the new house at Cope Place liveable in; Teresa, two dogs and I took refuge in Dolphin Square.

How I ever managed to look tidy for personal appearances I'll never know. The wardrobe was too small, an ironing-board was propped up in one corner, and I dragged clothes, as I needed them, from suitcases piled high in another.

It was during those hot summer months of total upheaval in 1977 that I decided to write my book. For ages lots of people had been on at me to put everything down on paper. Now I suppose I saw this as a form of escapism – and when I escape, I escape! Leaving Teresa and Joanie to cope with everything at home and Bunny Lewis to refuse all the work offered, I upped and left to spend three months in ... Singapore.

I chose the Far East because a mutual friend had introduced me to the brilliant miniaturist and artist, W.P. Mundy. And Bill, who was then still Managing Director of the Grant Kenyon Advertising Agency in Singapore, offered to arrange for me to stay with a delightful Chinese family, the Lims. 'You'll have absolute peace and quiet, and I'll be around if you need me,' was what he said.

So, with my typewriter uncovered, my paper and pens stacked, my research spread impressively around me, and my other problems back in England firmly to one side, I was all set to write a book!

Suddenly I discovered that, with no deadlines to meet and the lifting of all everyday pressures, my self-discipline, that self-discipline

I'd always prided myself on, had totally vanished. The rain didn't help either. Not a friendly drizzle, not even the odd tropical storm, violent but passing – these were the thick, heavy, endless blankets of rain of the monsoon season.

This I had not bargained for, nor could I have imagined the desperately depressing effect of never seeing the sun, yet sweating night and day in the unbearably humid heat. It was a true Somerset Maugham setting and I found myself wallowing in the self-pity I had always sworn I would never give in to. In this frame of mind it was too easy to accept the welcome but disrupting invitations to escape from my writing.

Bill, of course, was wonderful. He telephoned non-stop, came to see me often, took me out and did everything he could to lift my gloom and encourage me to keep writing. But it was a meagre and muddled manuscript that I brought back to England with me. I have no regrets, though, and don't feel that the time I spent in the Far East was wasted. Because through Bill and the Lims, I met a number of people who became and have remained firm friends.

Amongst them was the larger-than-life Sultan of Johore (whose portrait Bill has painted no less than seven times). H.R.H., a very lively gentleman in his eighties, and his dark, enchantingly-beautiful second wife, Tunku Nora, immediately welcomed me warmly. Not only did they shower me with hospitality and kindness then, but the following year, when I went back to Singapore with a party of *TV Times* competition winners, H.R.H. invited us all over to Johore. He also insisted on guiding, in his silver Lamborghini, a large busful of us, so the prizewinners could go home and tell of a personally-conducted tour around his kingdom. When my charges had left, their Royal Highnesses asked me to spend a very happy week in the palace with them.

Back in England, I had plenty of excuses not to continue that book. There were still things to be finished in the house, work had accumulated, deadlines had to be met, and all the everyday pressures soon built up again. Always, however, I had this nagging, guilty feeling inside me. I can't bear to leave unfinished something I've started. At the same time I was fully aware that I wasn't going to get this book done on my own. But there again, I was absolutely determined that no 'ghost' would do the job for me.

So what was the answer, I really didn't know – until one evening soon after I'd got back from Singapore, two friends dropped in to see me – Dawn Allan and Ann Calvert. Ann was talking about giving up her job at St Bartholomew's Hospital and looking forward to a life of leisure. It was when she said that she didn't really know how she'd take to doing nothing that I started to think.

She and I got on beautifully from the word go, there was one of those 'on the same wave-length' feelings between us. What's more, I knew she'd worked on the *Daily Mirror* so I assumed she had some journalistic experience. Would she be the right person to help me? For a few days I mulled over the idea. What would she think of it?

There was only one way to find out – I picked up the telephone and dialled: 'This is quite incredible,' she said. 'I had such a vivid dream last night. You were here writing, and I was sitting talking to Greville' (she'd never even met him). 'I know it sounds quite nutty, but I'm not at all surprised you telephoned.'

And that is exactly how it happened. I had found someone interested in listening to this story and discussing it as I wrote. Oh yes, I have written every single word myself, but Ann has kept my butterfly mind on a chronological track. I am very grateful to her.

P.S.

The telephone rang. It was Charles Hickman: 'Kate, if you're free that evening, put down 15 March. I'd love you to come to my first night.' Charles was directing Agatha Christie's *A Murder is Announced* at the Vaudeville Theatre.

I was refusing all invitations because of writing this book, but Charles being such a dear friend I made this the one exception, and said I would really look forward to it.

When the time came, though, I was having such excruciating back trouble that I was on the point of calling Charles to say I just couldn't make it. But he telephoned first. He said the producer, Peter Saunders, had asked me and John Kerr (our mutual friend and my godson) to a small party he was giving in his office before the show. I hadn't the heart to cry off.

Peter Saunders was only a name to me. I knew he had produced everything from Shakespeare to musicals, but was inevitably best known for Agatha Christie's *The Mousetrap*, which is already not far off its thirtieth year – a world-wide record.

I was slightly surprised at his reaction when we met. As we shook hands, a definite electric shock went through me and he pulled back as though he'd felt it too. But perhaps he was just surprised to see someone he didn't know at his party, for he hadn't recognized me. We exchanged a few words, then other guests followed me in. We spoke little after that. I propped my painful back up against the impressive marble chimney-piece in his office and became engrossed in talking to Noël Coward's biographer, Cole Lesley. As I left, Peter Saunders made what I thought was the mundane remark 'I hope we'll meet again'. But I wasn't to know that the very next day he asked Charles for my telephone number in order to invite me to lunch.

There is no doubt whatsoever that the impact was immediate. And it took a very short time for Peter and I to realize that the chemistry between us was perfect.

We discovered we had been widowed roughly about the same time. Peter had been very happily married, and had nursed his wife devotedly through a long and painful kidney failure. Since her death, life had lost a lot of its interest for him. As for me, I had publicly and repeatedly stated I would never marry again. When I met Peter, I knew I had to change my mind.

The day after we decided to get married, I was worrying about how to get Greville's two wedding-rings off my finger. They still seemed so permanently fixed. I mentioned this to Ann. 'Don't worry,' she said, 'they'll come off when they're meant to.'

I went on with my writing. Later that afternoon, I was playing with my rings and to my astonishment, but not to Ann's, they both slipped off very easily.

There is also a mimosa tree in Peter's garden, which his wife planted as a seed from the South of France. This appeared to die with her. Now, suddenly, more than four years later, it has started to flourish and bloom again. We both know that she and Greville approve of our happiness.

I treasure Peter's calm and wisdom, his kindness, his deep understanding and also his tremendous sense of humour. He is indeed a gentle man.

He says he enjoys my interest in everything and everyone. He enjoys the way I answer his questions before he has finished, so that I end up answering something quite different from what he is asking. He likes slightly less – but accepts with amused tolerance – my habit of kissing him goodnight and, as he rolls over to go to sleep, saying brightly, 'Would you like to talk now?' He observes with gentle benevolence my mania for polishing the brass in the house every day. He has even accepted my dog Tessa, whom he has (with every justification) renamed Dracula. And he says that beyond everything else he loves my effervescence and my love of life and laughter. I think he must be prejudiced.

But perhaps, when all is said and done, we simply fell in love.

Peter and I were married quietly in Lausanne on 28 August 1979 (five months after we first met), with Margherita and Enrico as witnesses.

That was intended to be the final paragraph of the book. Everything neatly rounded off: 'and they lived happily ever after'. But it didn't happen quite that way. Three weeks after we were married, Peter was rushed to hospital with chest pains. The specialist told him the news and left him to break it to me.

'I've had a coronary. A mild one,' he added hastily.

'Oh, no, this can't be happening to me again,' I cried.

'Well, no, darling – in fact it's happening to me!'

This amazing husband of mine, even then, never lost either his cool or his dry sense of humour. But now, with Peter better and back at work, I cross my fingers and pray that this really is the final paragraph and that we *will* live happily ever after.

Index

Abba, 161
Acapulco, 163
Adams, Victor, 102
Adelaide, 118
Afton, Richard, 123–7
Aldwick Bay, 11
Alexander, General Sir
  Harold (later Earl), 6
Allan, Dawn, 187
Allen, Steve, 173
Amodio, Julio de, 93
Antonio (Spanish
  dancer), 158
Armagh, 92
Ascot, 135, 136
Ashe Park, 91, 103
Ashley, Iris, 138
Askey, Arthur, 145

Bacigalupo, Dottoressa,
  53
Back, Barbara, 89–90
Bardonecchia, 29–31
Barker, Eric, 126
Barnes, Binnie, 97
Barnett, Isobel, 128

Barr, Patrick, 152
Barraclough, Judy, 116
Basra, 114
Baylis, Catherine, 141
Baylis, Greville (second
  husband), 124, 129,
  145–6, 150, 151–2,
  153, 157, 161, 181–2,
  189; first meeting,
  113; growing
  friendship, 118, 119–
  22, 123, 130–9; horse-
  racing, 134–7;
  divorce from second
  wife, 138–9; marriage
  to Katie, 140–1;
  holidays, 147–9, 166–
  7, 177; extramarital
  affairs, 154–5, 160,
  163–5; accident and
  death, 166–74;
  communication after
  death, 177–80
Baylis, Jean, 120, 131,
  132, 135, 137
Baylis, Mark, 120,
  141

Baylis, Pat Maxwell,
  120, 141
Baylis, Samantha, 141
Becker, Sir Walter, 6–7,
  9
Becker, Lady – see
  Imperiali dei Principi
  di Francavilla
Bell, Jean, 104, 105
Bellaigue, Toinon,
  Vicomtesse de, 103
Bellairs, Bice, 100–102
Bellaria, 21
Belper, Alexander
  Strutt, 4th Baron, 135
Benham, Joan, 152
Bentine, Michael, 143
Berlin, 17–18
Bertalazona, Villa, 68–
  74, 75, 76–7, 92
Bieber, Kay, 132–3
Birmingham, 143
Blanc, Giuseppe, 23
Blanc, Isa, 108
Blanc, Orazio, 23, 29–
  32, 97, 107, 108
Bognor Regis, 11–12

Bombay, 121–2
Boon Haw, A.W., 116
Borovski, Natasha, 14
Boyd, Alan, 104
Boyer, Jacqueline, 157
Boyle, Patrick (now
    Earl of Cork and
    Orrery) (stepfather),
    94, 107, 123, 179–80
Boyle, Richard,
    Viscount (now Earl of
    Shannon) (first
    husband), 94, 102,
    106–7, 110–12, 113,
    123, 140, 145; first
    meeting, 90;
    marriage, 91–2; army
    postings, 92–3, 103,
    107; increasing
    incompatibility, 108–
    9, 112, 120–1;
    separation and three-
    year plan, 129, 131,
    137; divorce, 138–9
Brambell, Wilfrid, 152
Brighton, 160–1
Brillantmont, Villa
    (Lausanne), 14–15, 17,
    18
Brisson, Carl, 124
Broadstairs, 12–13
Brocas-Burrows,
    General, 107
Bromborough, 153–4
Brook, Clive, 148–9
Brook, Faith, 152
Brooke, Millie, 148
Bruce, Brenda, 126
Buchanan, Jack, 145
Budapest, 7, 8
Bunting, Patience, 181
Butlin, Billy, 149

Cabrini, Collegio
    (Genoa), 20–21, 26
Cairo, 114
Calvert, Ann, 179, 187,
    189
Campbell, Donald and
    Dorothy, 125
Campbell-Walter, Fiona
    (Baroness Thyssen),
    126
Cardiff, 171–2
Cargill, Patrick, 102
Carnarvon, Henry
    Herbert, 6th Earl of,
    135
Carroll, Ronnie, 158
Carter, Ernestine, 138
Casanova, Baron, 125
'Caterina' (racehorse),
    136
Cattle, Peter, 172
Ceylon (now Sri
    Lanka), 114–15, 119–
    21
Chiari, Walter, 158
Christian, Linda (Blanca
    Rosa Welter), 23–4,
    97, 98
Clark, Peter, 104
Cohen, Renato, 45
Coin-Op Dry-Cleaning,
    153–4
Connor, Kenneth, 143
Cooke, Peta and Tony,
    135
Coombs, Pat, 125
Cooper, Gladys, 145
Cooper, Rosemary,
    112, 113, 114, 118
Cordiglia,
    Commendatore and
    Signora, 73–5

Counsell, John, 98–100
Coward, Noël, 145
Crazy Gang, 145
Creighton-Blair, Gillian
    (Mrs Richard Afton),
    125

Damone, Franco, 46–7,
    48, 50, 51–2, 53, 58,
    72, 178; growing
    affection between
    Katie and, 49; affair,
    55–6, 57, 59–60, 85;
    with Katie in Turin
    hideaway, 63–4;
    arrest by partisans,
    64; execution,
    66
Damone, Signora, 47,
    63, 70
D'Aria, Father, 26–7
Darwin, 116
Dauberson, Dany,
    108
Dawnay, Jean (now
    Princess George
    Galitzine), 114, 118
Delmitia, Villa
    (Rapallo), 9, 42, 50
Denison, Michael, 145
Denney, Anthony, 112,
    114, 118
Diani Beach, 165, 166–
    70
Dick Whittington
    (Windsor
    pantomime), 102
Dietrich, Maria, 14
Dietrich, Marlene, 14–
    15
Dunlop, John, 135

INDEX

Eastwood, Bill and
  Dorothy, 153, 154,
  164
Edinburgh, 134
Elstree Studios, 94
Elvin, Violetta, 125
Epernay, 143
European Radio and
  Television Personality
  of the Year, 158
European Song Contest,
  151, 154, 156–62

Falkender, Lady, 183–4
Farina, Pinin, 8
'Fast and Friendly'
  (racehorse), 136
Field, Peggy, 184
Fiesole, 3
Fiorita, Villa (near
  Fiesole), 3, 4
Flanagan, Alan, 167,
  168, 170
Flanagan, Anne, 167,
  170
Flanagan, Bud, 145
Florence, 1, 2–3, 4, 6,
  19–20, 28, 45; Poggio
  Imperiale, 22–5
Freeman, Alan, 141
Fricker, Edward, 182–3
Friedlander, Carl and
  Louise, 133–4
Fusco, Mother, 28–9

Galloway, John and Joy,
  113
Gammell, Fenella, 12,
  13
Garland, Judy, 97

Garnier, Mother, 27
Geneave, Norma, 116
Geneva, 145
Genoa, 20, 36
Gethin, Ken, 136
Gigli, Beniamino, 19–20
Gilbey, Quinney, 135
Gleneagles, 142
Gloucester, Prince
  Henry, Duke of, 82
Goalen, Barbara, 105,
  117
'Golden Girl', 152
Goller, Dr, 104
Goodson & Todman,
  127
Goodwood, 136
Goons, the, 143–4
Granville, Lord, 92
Gray, Dulcie, 145
Greater London Fund
  for the Blind, 84, 184
Green, Felicity, 138

Hackney, Pearl, 126
Hall, Ray, 173
Hambledon, Viscountess
  (Maria Carmela
  Attolico), 32
Hamond-Graeme, Sir
  Egerton and Lady, 84
Handl, Irene, 125
Harding, Gilbert, 128–
  9, 139
Harewood, George
  Lascelles, 7th Earl of,
  116
Hartnell, Sir Norman,
  134, 142
Hawkins, Doreen, 98
Hawkins, Jack, 97

Heath, Ted, 145
Henson, Leslie, 145
Heubi, Mlle, 14
Hickman, Charles, 152,
  153, 188, 189
Hilton, Ronnie, 125
Holland, Canon Henry
  Scott, 175, 180
Holliday, Michael, 124
Hope, Bob, 145
Howerd, Frankie, 145
Huguenin, M. and
  Mme, 14
Hvoshinsky-Gortcha-
  kov, Prince and
  Princess, 2
Hylton, Jack, 145

Imperiali dei Principi di
  Francavilla, Marchesa
  Augusta (stepmother),
  42–3, 48, 56–7, 58,
  60, 66, 70, 75, 110,
  111, 146, 150
Imperiali dei Principi di
  Francavilla, Marchesa
  Delphine ('God-
  mother')
  (stepmother), 6, 17,
  18–19, 21, 29, 30, 34,
  35–6, 37, 42, 44, 47,
  49, 81, 83; marriage
  to Imperiali, 7–8;
  close relationship with
  Katie, 8–9, 41, 50;
  operation for breast
  cancer, 39–41;
  recurrence of illness,
  50–51, 52; forced to
  alter will, 51, 52;
  death, 53

Imperiali dei Principi di Francavilla, Marchese Demetrio (father), 3–9, 14, 15–18, 22, 29, 30, 32, 34, 37, 38–43, 72, 76, 81, 91; background, 2; separation from first wife, 5; Fascism, 6; second marriage, 7–8; and Katie's education, 11, 12, 13, 18–19, 20, 25; musical evenings, 19, 35–6; megalomania, 41, 50; wartime political dealings, 43, 44–5, 46–7, 48–50, 57–8, 66, 67; 'reign of terror', 51–3, 54, 55; liaison and third marriage, 56–7, 58–9, 70, 75; imprisonment of Katie, 58–9, 61, 66, 67, 70; desertion of her, 75; reunion in England, 109–12; second family, 110, 111, 145, 146; later meeting in Switzerland, 145–6; death, 150

Imperiali dei Principi di Francavilla, Marchesa Dorothy (mother), 3–7, 22, 29, 70, 74, 88, 96, 113; background, 2–3; birth of Katie, 4; separation from husband, 5; and Katie's education, 11, 13, 18–19; in Switzerland with second husband, 51; reunion with Katie, 76–80, 92; plans for Katie's London life, 80–82, 85, 87; return to Switzerland, 86; and Katie's first marriage, 91, 92, 106–7; marriage to Patrick Boyle, 123, 179; last years, 180

Imperiali dei Principi di Francavilla, Marchese Enrico (grandfather), 2

Imperiali dei Principi di Francavilla, Enrico (half-brother), 110, 111, 145, 173, 190

Imperiali dei Principi di Francavilla, Marchesa Katia ('Nonna') (grandmother), 2, 3, 15, 20, 36–8, 48, 54, 57, 58

Imperiali dei Principi di Francavilla, Margherita (half-sister), 110, 111, 145, 173, 190

Ingham, Stafford, 135, 136

Intent to Kill (film), 152

Irene of Greece, Princess (later Duchess of Spoleto), 4, 24

Ischia, 140

'I've Got a Secret', 151

Ivor Novello Awards, 149–50

Jackson, Winifride, 138

Jacques, David, 179

Jeanmaire, Zizi, 158

Joan ('daily'), 103, 129, 172, 174, 185

Johore, Sultan of, 186

Josephine of the Belgians, Princess, 28

Judd, Edward, 152

Keel, Howard, 145

Kelly, Barbara, 128

Kelly, Elizabeth, 87

Kerr, Annabel, 92

Kerr, Sir Howard, 82, 102, 123

Kerr, Christine, Lady, 82, 102

Kerr, Lord John, 84, 86

Kerr, Marie, 82, 83–4

Kerridge, Mary, 98

Kokoschka, Oskar, 42

Kuala Lumpur, 119

Langton, David, 152

Lausanne, 2, 14, 79–81, 190

Lawrence, Gertrude, 14

Lawrence, Pamela, 14

Lawton, Frank, 152

Laye, Evelyn, 152, 153

Leeds Castle, 143

Legge, Mrs Gerald, 104

Leopold III of the Belgians, 28

Lesley, Cole, 189

Lester, Dick, 144

Lewis, Bunny, 147, 172, 173, 185

Lewis, Janique, 147

Lewis, Michael, 104
Lim family, 185, 186
Lime Grove, 124, 137
Lipyeat, Queenie, 147, 160
Littlewood Songsters, 125
Llandudno, 153, 154
Lohr, Marie, 152
Lothian, Peter Kerr, Marquess of, 83
Lothian, Antonella (Toni), Marchioness of, 84, 184
Lucan, Arthur, 94

Macdonald, Anne, 95, 96, 97, 100, 102
McEwan, Geraldine, 102
McGivern, Cecil, 137
Margaret, Princess, 92, 143
Maria José, Crown Princess of Italy, 28
Martin, Millicent, 158
Mascagni, Pietro, 24
Matthews, Francis, 152
Melbourne, 117
'Melody Fare', 181
Milland, Muriel (Mal), 98
Milland, Ray, 97
Milligan, Spike, 143
Mirman, Serge and Simone, 104–5
Moet & Chandon, 143
Mombasa, 165, 168, 169
Montallegro, Sanctuary of (near Rapallo), 41
Montand, Yves, 158

Montego Bay, 132, 133
More, Kenneth, 158
Morris, Stewart, 159
Mortlock, Joyce, 161
Mouskouri, Nana, 158
Muir, Frank, 126, 127
Mundy, W.P., 185, 186
Munro, Matt, 149
Murder is Announced, A (Christie), 188
Murray, Ruby, 124
Mussolini, Benito, 6, 44, 47

'Name's the Same, The', 126, 127
Naples, 140
Nelson, Peter and Mackie, 135
New York, 133–4, 151
Newmarket, 136
Newton John, Olivia, 162
Nicholls, Tigie and Tom, 135
Nichols, Beverly, 89–90
Nissim, Elio, 111, 112
Norden, Denis, 126
Norfolk, Lavinia, Duchess of, 135
Nostell Priory, 142

O'Hara, Mary, 124
O'Keefe, Declan, 169
O'Shea, Kitty, 94
O'Sullevan, Peter, 135, 137
Oake, Della, 114, 118

Oboukhoff, Lily, 36–7, 48, 54, 57, 58
Oboukhoff, Nadine, 36–8, 48, 54, 57, 58
Ocho Rios, 132–3
Ofarim, Esther, 158
Olga, Princess de Hesse, 14

Packer, John, 142
Paris, 15–17, 107–8
Parnell, Charles, 119
Parnell, Laura, 114, 115, 118–20, 121, 122
Patrick, Nigel, 145
Pecorella, Dottore, 76–7, 96
Phillips, S.J., 159
'Plymouth Fair' (racehorse), 135
Poggio Imperiale (Florence), 22–5
Pond's, 104
'Pop Over Europe', 173
Pound, Ezra, 42
Power, Tyrone, 13, 24, 97
Price, Will, 122
Proops, Marjorie, 138
Pye TV Awards, 183

Queen Charlotte Ball, 84
'Quite Contrary', 183, 124–6, 127, 137

Ramsden, Arthur (great-uncle), 3
Ramsden, Jim (uncle), 2

Ramsden, Kate ('Gaggie') (grandmother), 2, 3, 11

Ramsden, Robert (grandfather), 2

Randolph, Elsie, 145

Rapallo, 8, 9, 29, 41–2, 45, 47, 52–4

Read, Al, 145

Redmond, Moira, 152

Regan, Joan, 124

Reid & Taylor Spectaculars, 142

Rennie, Michael, 97

Réthy, Princesse de, 28

Richard, Cliff, 149, 159

'Richer' (racehorse), 135–6

Richmond, 110

Rickatson-Hatt, Bernard, 109–10

Roberts, Paddy, 149

Robinson, Eric, 157

Rogers, Harry, 181

Rome, 78, 96–7, 114; Convent of the Sacred Heart, 25–9, 32, 96, 140–1

Rook, Jean, 138

Rosebery, Harry Primrose, 6th Earl of, 135

Rosebery, Eva, Lady, 135

Royal Variety Performance (1954), 145

Rozel Bay, 92

Rutland, Anne, Duchess of, 126

'Sally Rose' (racehorse), 135

San Maurizio Canavese, 67

Sanga, Mother, 140

Saunders, Ann, 189

Saunders, Peter (third husband), 188–90

Scammell, Karen, 116

Scelsi, Giacinto (stepfather), 51, 78, 79, 81, 86, 96

Scofield, Paul, 102

Scopoli, Signora, 23, 24–5

Secombe, Harry, 143–4

Sellers, Peter, 143, 144

Shannon, Robert Boyle, 8th Earl of, 90, 91

Shannon, Marjorie, Countess of, 91

Shapiro, Helen, 149

Shaw, Sandie, 159

Sheriffe, Monica, 135

Shmith, Bambi (now Countess of Harewood), 116

Silver Wedding (Clayton-Hutton), 152–3

Singapore, 115–16, 119, 185–6

Sloan, Tom, 146–7, 152, 156, 157, 160

Smith-Bingham, Arthur, 120

Smythe, Ted, 135

Sophie, Queen of Greece, 4

Sorrento, 6

Sri Lanka (Ceylon), 114–15, 119–21

Stark, Graham, 143, 144

Starke, Frederick, 117

Stiebel, Victor, 125, 145

Sunday Graphic, 138

'Susannah' (racehorse), 135

Sutherland, Joan, 158

Swanson, Gloria, 97

Swerling, the Misses, 89

Sydney, 116–17

Tache, Anne Marie, 110, 111, 112, 145

Tam, Professor, 68, 70, 73, 76

Taylor, Captain Tom, 74–5, 76

Teasy Weasy, Mr, 125

Television Toppers, 125

Teresa (housekeeper), 165, 172, 173, 174, 185

'That Was the Week That Was', 158

Thélin, Mother de, 25

Throckmorton, Sir Robert, 120

Tobago, 148–9, 150

Todd, Richard, 152

Tree, Jeremy, 136

Trehearne, Anne, 130

Truman, Margaret, 151

Turin, 6, 8, 9, 19, 33, 57, 60, 63–6, 74, 77

TV Times, 163, 164, 175

Valente, Caterina, 158

Valentine, Dickie, 145

Valsalice (near Turin), 8, 18–19, 25, 33–41, 45–52, 54–63, 66–7
Venice, 143, 158–9
Ventura, Dolores, 124
Vise, Tanse, 158
Vogue, 112, 118

Ward, Stephen, 97
Weedon, Bert, 125
'What's My Line?', 127, 151
Whitehanger Nursing Home, 180
Whittaker, Michael, 134

Willoughby de Broke, Lord and Lady, 135
Wilson, Mary, Lady, 184
Wilson, Pat, 162
Windsor Theatre Royal, 98–102
Winnick, Maurice, 127, 137
Winstone, Myrtle, 176–7
Wisdom, Norman, 145
Wogan, Terry, 162
Wolfit, Donald, 145
'Woman of the Year' Luncheon, 84, 184

Woman's Own, 89
Wontner, Sir Hugh, 130
Woolworth's, 173
Wurmser, Alfred, 157

Yamada, Senta, 181

Zeggio, Baron, 45
Zulueta, Ann de, 86
Zulueta, Dora de, 86
Zulueta, Peter de, 86
Zulueta, Philip de, 86
Zulueta, Father Philip de, 91